PYTHON PROGRAMMING

3 Books in 1

THE COMPLETE BEGINNER'S GUIDE TO LEARNING THE MOST POPULAR PROGRAMMING LANGUAGE.

By: Dylan Penny

Python Programming

© Copyright 2020 - All rights reserved.

The content contained within this book may not be reproduced, duplicated or transmitted without direct written permission from the author or the publisher.

Under no circumstances will any blame or legal responsibility be held against the publisher, or author, for any damages, reparation, or monetary loss due to the information contained within this book. Either directly or indirectly.

Legal Notice:

This book is copyright protected. This book is only for personal use. You cannot amend, distribute, sell, use, quote or paraphrase any part, or the content within this book, without the consent of the author or publisher.

Disclaimer Notice:

Please note the information contained within this document is for educational and entertainment purposes only. All effort has been executed to present accurate, up to date, and reliable, complete information. No warranties of any kind are declared or implied. Readers acknowledge that the author is not engaging in the rendering of legal, financial, medical or professional advice. The content within this book has been derived from various sources. Please consult a licensed professional before attempting any techniques outlined in this book.

By reading this document, the reader agrees that under no circumstances is the author responsible for any losses, direct or indirect, which are incurred as a result of the use of information contained within this document, including, but not limited to, — errors, omissions, or inaccuracies.

"Python" and the Python Logo are trademarks of the Python Software Foundation.

```
No portion of this book may be reproduced in any form without
written permission from the publisher or author, except as
permitted by U.S. copyright law.
```

Table Of Contents

Tuples .... ??
Objects .... ??
Introduction 1
Copyright .... ??
Common Uses of Python 4
Common Uses of Python 4

Chapter - 1 Python Basics 7
Install Python 8
Basic Python Types 14
Naming Styles 14
Python Variables 15
Variable vs. Constants 16
Naming Variables 16
Python Numbers 17
Integer Example 18
Float Example 18
Float and Integer Example 18
Complex Number Example 19
Python Strings 19
String Example 19
Python Boolean 20
Python Collections 21
Python Lists 21
Python Tuples 23
Python Sets 24
Python Dictionaries 24
Determining Type 25
Digging Deeper Into Python Strings 25
Python String Methods 28
Splitting a String Apart 29
Counting Characters in a String 30
Replace Part of a String 30
Removing White Space From Begin/End of String 31
Joining Strings 31
String Tests 32
Starts With & Ends With Test 32

Other String Tests	33
Digging Deeper Into Python Booleans	33
Digging Deeper into Python Lists	35
Creating a List	35
Element at Index	36
Element at Negative Index	37
Extracting Part of a List	37
Extracting the First Elements of a List	38
Extracting the Last Elements of a List	38
Changing Element in a List	39
Determining Length of a List	40
Appending to a List	40
Copying Existing Python List	41
Deleting Element from List	42
Concatenation of Lists	44
List Exercises	45
How to Organize a List	48
Sorting Number Lists	49
Sorting String Lists	51
Digging Deeper into Python Tuples	54
Creating a Tuple	55
Extracting an Element from a Tuple	55
Extracting an Element from the End of a Tuple	56
Extracting Elements from a Tuple	56
Extracting Elements from the End of a Tuple	57
Workaround for Modifying Tuple	57
Length of a Tuple	58
Deletion Rules of a Tuple	59
Joining Tuples	59
Tuple Exercises	60
Digging Deeper into Python Sets	61
Creating a Set	62
Adding Elements to Set	63
Adding Elements to Set with Update()	63
Determining the Length of a Set	64
Selectively Delete an Element from a Set	64
Delete the Entire Set	66
Delete All the Contents of a Set	66
Set Exercises	68
Digging Deeper into Python Dictionaries	70
Creating a Python Dictionary	71
How to Change Values in a Python Dictionary	72

How To Loop Through a Python Dictionary 73
Print the Key Names in a Dictionary: 73
Print the Values in a Dictionary: 74
Print the Keys and Values in a Dictionary: 75
Check if a Key Exists in the Dictionary 76
How To Determine Number of Items in Dictionary 76
Add an Item to the Python Dictionary 77
Removing Items from the Python Dictionary 77
List of Common Python Dictionary Methods 81
Advantages of a Python Dictionary 81
Disadvantages of a Python Dictionary 82
Digging Deeper into Python Numbers 83
Basic Python Numerical Operators 83
Python Operators 83
Python Arithmetic Operators 83
Python Comparison Operators 87
Python Assignment Operators 90
Python Bitwise Operators 92
Python Logical Operator 94
Python Membership Operator 95
Python Identity Operators 96
Python Operator Precedence 98
Conditionals 99
If Statements 99
Python Indentation 99
Types of Conditional If Statements in Python 101
If Statement 101
If-else Statement 103
if-elif-else Statement 104
Functions 107
Print Output 115
Input and Output 118
Loops in Python 123
For Loops 124
While Loops 133
Python Modules 135
Objects, Methods, and Inheritance 142
Classes and Objects 143
Review 155
Conclusion 157

Chapter - 2 Python For Data Analysis 159

Why Python for Data Analysis? 160
Data Analysis - The Basics 162
Data Analysis Process 167
Essential Python Libraries 170
Data Analysis Python Libraries 176
Python Installation and Setup 181
LPython and Jupyter Notebooks 190
NumPy Basics 202
Getting Started with Pandas 213
Plotting and Visualization 225
Data Aggregation and Grouping 233
Modeling Libraries in Python 238
Conclusion 243

Chapter - 3 Python For Data Science **246**
Introduction 247
Basic Python For Data Science 251
Machine Learning 257
Statistics and Probabilities 262
Data Science Algorithms and Models 274
Neural Network 296
Deep Learning vs. Machine Learning 303
Conclusion 317

Dylan Penny

Introduction

Companies have spent a lot of time investigating data analysis and what it can do for them. Data surrounds us and it each day, more new information is available for us to work with. Whether you are a business trying to gain insights in your industry and your customers or just an individual who has a question about a certain topic, you will be able to find a wealth of information to help you get started.

Many companies have started gathering up data and leveraging it for their needs. They find insights and predictions inside this data to make future decisions. Data, properly used can help our business become more successful.

Gathering the data is only the first step and there is more work to do. Additional work is required to see what patterns are inside. This is where Data Analysis is going to come into play to reveal those patterns.

To take this a bit further, data analysis is going to be a practice where we can take some of the raw data that our business has been collecting, and then organize and re-order it into something useful.

For example, when you run data analysis on your customers, you may find that a certain type of customer tends to buy another product from you. This would prompt you to email the customers an offer to buy the product and maybe expand your lineup with similar products.

The one thing that we need to be careful about the way that we manipulate the data that we have. It is really to manipulate the data in the wrong way during the analysis phase and then end up pushing certain conclusions or agendas that are not there. This is why we need to pay close attention when the data analysis is presented to us and think critically about the data and the conclusions drawn from the data.

If you are worried about a source or if you are not sure that you are able to complete the analysis without some biases, then it is important to find someone else to work on it or choose a different source. There is a lot of data available to generate reports, but you have to be careful about these biases. They could lead us to the wrong decisions if we are not careful.

In addition, you will find that during the data analysis, the raw data that you will work with can take on a variety of forms. This can include things like observations, survey responses, and measurements, to name a few. The sources that you use for this kind of raw data will vary based on what you are hoping to get out of it, what your main question is all about, and more.

In its raw form, the data that we are gathering is going to be very useful to work with, but you may find that it is a bit overwhelming to work with as well. This is a problem that a lot of companies are going to have and you will gain experience and intuition as you work in this area.

Over the time that you gather data and through all of the steps in the process, the raw data will become ordered in a useful manner. For example, we may send out a survey and then tally up the results from the survey. Even the basic data helps us to see at a glance how many people decided to answer the survey at all, and how people were willing to respond to some of the specific questions that were on that survey.

In the process of collating and organizing the data, a trend is likely going to emerge, and sometimes more than one trend. We are going to highlight these trends, usually in the write-up that is being done on the data. These trends need to be highlighted to ensure the person who is reading that information pays attention to the trends.

There are a lot of places that we are going to see this. For example, in a casual kind of survey, you may want to figure out the preferences between men and women of what ice cream flavors they prefer. In this survey, maybe we find out that women and men are going to favor chocolate. Depending on who is using this information and what they are hoping to get out of that information, it could be something that the researcher can highlight. At a meeting with these people, make sure there are different chocolates to nibble on.

Modeling the data from the survey, or out of another form of data analysis, using mathematics and other tools, can sometimes exaggerate the points of interest in our data, which is going to make it easier for anyone who is looking over the data, especially the researcher, to see trends early.

In addition to taking a look at all of the data that you have collected and sorted through, you will need to do a few other parts as well. These are all meant to help the person who needs this information understand it, digest it and make conclusions from the data.

This means that we need to spend our time discussing how to describe the data, graphs, charts, and other ways to represent and show the data to those who need it. This will be one of the final steps in data analysis. We will discuss techniques to distill and refine the data for our readers and customers.

Summarizing the data in these steps is going to be critical, and it needs to be done well. This is critical to supporting the arguments that are made with that data, as is presenting the data clearly and understandably. During this phase, remember that the person who needs that summary and who will use it to make some important decisions for the business is probably not a data scientists and they need the conclusions written out in a simple and easy to understand way.

Often this is going to be done with some sort of data visualization. There are many choices of visuals that we can work with and working with graphs or charts is a good option as well. Working with the data everyday will help you think of ways to deliver the information through visuals.

Many times, reading through information in a more graphical format is easier than just reading through the data and understanding the obvious information. To see those complex relationships quickly and efficiently, working with a visual is one of the best options.

Even though we will focus our work on converting the raw information into visual data to make it easier to work with and understand, it is recommended to add the raw data in the appendix, rather than just throwing it out. This allows the person who is going to work with that data regularly a chance to check your sources and your specific numbers and can help to bolster some of the results that you are getting overall.

If you are the one who is getting the results of the data analysis, make sure that when you get the conclusions and the summarized data from your data scientist that you go through and view them more critically. You should ask where the data comes from and you should also ask about the method of sampling that was used as well as when the data was collected. Knowing the size of the sample is important as well.

Common Uses of Python

According to recent reports, Python is used by around 1.5 million developers. Many sites, APIs, and programs are built using Python.

Python's popularity is a direct result of its open-source nature that encourages software engineers to use and share their programs.

Don't dismiss Python as simply a scripting language. Python is promoted as a multiuse language suitable for many clients and applications.

Here are some global organizations that utilization Python for their items:
- Google broadly utilizes Python to construct and update its web index crawlers.
- YouTube was initially built on Python. A great deal of YouTube's ability to quickly change and adapt can be credited to Python.
- Netflix uses Python for "Suggested for You" metrics.
- Dropbox, a storage tool, utilizes Python to scramble the records.

Here are some specialized fields where Python is widely utilized:

Systems Programming

This is a part of software engineering where we create frameworks for hardware devices, for example, compilers, translators, and shell instruments that are used for testing. Python's versatility is perfect for this task because it has many useful testing libraries and frameworks.

Internet

Python is useful for making websites or APIs using Flask or Django frameworks.

Python is also popular for creating web applications that can store sensitive data. There is a large community of WebCrawler and website admins using Python to configure and monitor their applications.

Database Programming

Databases are the preferred method to store and control data. There are many database query languages to store and retrieve information but Python is flexible and can be quickly modified. As a result, Python is used by numerous database admins to interact with databases.

A program can be written using Python libraries to monitor for infections and store a database backup in the remote server.

Machine Learning

Artificial Intelligence (AI) is an exploding software engineering field for examining and learning from the data and information that is available. Python has popular libraries (ie. SciPy and Pandas) for manipulating data for use in AI and Machine Learning.

What Are Python's Qualities?

Python is commonly recommended for novices since it contains all the basic structures that programming languages use.

Many central programming concepts (ie. Conditional program flow, variables, types and classes) are learned while programming in Python.

Open-source

Python is continually enhanced by contributors from all around the world. This collaboration makes it easier to create programs and distribute these new concepts.

This open-source nature lets software engineers try different things with the code and make some creative applications.

Powerful

Python is ground-breaking when compared to other well-known programming languages. The simplicity of the language means developers can quickly prototype and proof of concept and test it.

Python utilizes a garbage collector to clean memory during operation. Less time spent worrying about releasing memory properly means more time available for programming..

Default Instruments

Python offers a great deal of extremely helpful framework instruments. It can play out a ton of string activities effectively utilizing these default devices. It is additionally imperative to comprehend these modules to perform tasks in a superior manner utilizing Python.

CHAPTER - 1

Python Basics

Install Python

To code in Python, you must have the Python Interpreter installed on your computer. You must also have a text editor to write and save your Python programs. The good thing with Python is that it can run on various platforms like Windows, Linux, and Mac OS. Most of the current versions of these operating systems come installed with Python. You can check whether Python has been installed on your operating system by running this command on the terminal or operating system console:

```
python --version
```

Type the above command on the Terminal of your operating system, then hit the Enter/Return key.

The command should return the version of Python installed on your system. If Python is not installed, you will be informed that the command is not recognized; indicating you have to install Python.

Choosing a Python Version

The main two versions of Python are 2.x and 3.x. Python 3.x is obviously the latest one and will continue growing much faster in terms of adoption. The advice for you is to start with the latest version Python 3.x. because starting in 2020 Python 2.x is not supported anymore.

General Installations Instruction

Installing Python is very easy. All you need to do is follow the steps described below:

1. Go to Python downloads page https://www.python.org/downloads/
2. Click the link related to your operating system

> Looking for Python with a different OS? Python for Windows, Linux/UNIX, Mac OS X, Other

3. Click on the latest release and download according to your operating system
4. Launch the package and follow the installation instructions (we recommend to leave the default settings)

Make sure you click on "**Add Python 3.x to PATH**". Once the installation is finished, you are set to go!

The following instructions are OS specific.

Installation on Windows

To install Python on Windows, download Python from its official website, then double click the downloaded setup package to launch the installation. You can download the package by clicking this link:

https://www.python.org/downloads/windows/

It will be good for you to download and install the latest package of Python as you will be able to enjoy using the latest Python packages. After downloading the package, double click on it, and you will be guided through on-screen instructions on how to install Python on your Windows OS.

Installation on Linux (Ubuntu)

In Linux, there are several package managers that can be used for the installation of Python in various Linux distributions. For example, if you are using Ubuntu Linux, run this command to install Python:

$ sudo apt-get install python3-minimal

Python will be installed on your system. However, most of the latest versions of various Linux distributions come installed with Python. Just run the "python" command. If you get a Python version as the return, then Python has been installed on your system. If not, go ahead and install Python.

Installation on Mac OS

To install Python in Mac OS, you must first download the package. You can find it by opening the following link on your web browser:

https://www.python.org/downloads/mac-osx/

After the setup has been downloaded, double click it to launch the installation. You will be presented with on-screen instructions that will guide you through the installation process. Lastly, you will have Python running on your Mac OS system.

Testing the Installation

1. Start the Python IDLE (Integrated Development and Learning Environment). On Linux and Mac, you do this by typing "python" in the Terminal

```
$ python3
Python 3.9.13 (main, May 24 2022, 21:28:31)
[Clang 13.1.6 (clang-1316.0.21.2)] on darwin
Type "help", "copyright", "credits" or "license" for more information.
>>>
```

You can type simple Python commands after the ">>>" and they will execute immediately.

Prove that everything works by writing your first Python code:

```
$ python3
Python 3.9.13 (main, May 24 2022, 21:28:31)
[Clang 13.1.6 (clang-1316.0.21.2)] on darwin
Type "help", "copyright", "credits" or "license" for more information.
>>> print("I'm running my first Python code")
I'm running my first Python code
>>>
```

Press enter or return; this is what you should get:

```
>>> print ("I'm running my first Python code")
I'm running my first Python code
```

You can do the same also by launching this command using a file. We will address this after we address the Python IDLE or another code editor.

More About Running Programs

One can run Python programs in two main ways:

Python Programming

- Interactive interpreter
- Script from the command line

Interactive Interpreter or Interactive Mode via Shell

Python comes with a command-line, which is commonly referred to as the interactive interpreter. You can write your Python code directly on this interpreter and press the enter key. You will get instant results. If you are on Linux, you only have to open the Linux terminal, then type "python." Hit the enter key, and you will be presented with the Python interpreter with the >>> symbol. To access the interactive Python interpreter on Windows, click Start -> All programs, then identify "Python ..." from the list of programs. In my case, I find "Python 3.5" as I have installed Python 3.5. Expand this option and click "Python ..." In my case, I click "Python 3.5(64-bit)," and I get the interactive Python interpreter.

```
Python 3.5 (64-bit)
Python 3.5.0 (v3.5.0:374f501f4567, Sep 13 2015, 02:27:37) [MSC v.1900 64 bit (AMD64)] on win32
Type "help", "copyright", "credits" or "license" for more information.
>>>
```

Here, you can write and run your Python scripts directly. To write the "Hello" example, type the following on the interpreter terminal:

>>> *print("Hello")*

Hit the enter/return key, and the text "Hello" will be printed on the interpreter:

> *$ python3*
> *Python 3.9.13 (main, May 24 2022, 21:28:31)*
> *[Clang 13.1.6 (clang-1316.0.21.2)] on darwin*
> *Type "help", "copyright", "credits" or "license" for more information.*
> *>>> print ("Hello")*
> *Hello*
> *>>> print("Hello")*

Script from Command Line

This method involves writing Python programs in a file, then invoking the Python interpreter to work on the file. Files with Python should be saved with a .py extension. This is a designation to signify that it is a Python file. For example, script.py, myscript.py, etc. After writing your code in the file and saving it with the name "mycode.py," you can open the operating system command line and invoke the Python interpreter to work on the file. For example, you can run this command on the command line to execute the code on the file mycode.py:

> *$ python3 mycode.py*

The Python interpreter will work on the file and print the results on the terminal.

Python IDE (Integrated Development Environment)

If you have a GUI (Graphical User Interface) application capable of supporting Python, you can run Python on a GUI environment. The following are the Python IDEs for the various operating systems:

- UNIX- IDLE
- Windows-PythonWin

Macintosh comes along with IDLE IDE, downloadable from the official website as MacBinary or BinHex'd files.

Basic Python Types

Python supports different data types which is a way of grouping information. Variables are storage containers for data. How would we describe a group of students? One way would be describing them by name (we would use 'name' as a variable). Another way to describe the students would be by age (we would use 'age' as the variable).

Each variable should belong to one of the data types supported in Python. The data type determines the value that can be assigned to a variable, the type of operation that may be applied to the variable as well as the amount of space assigned to the variable.

Naming Styles

A variable must be a single word without spaces but it can use underscores (such as 'student_age') or a word made up of many smaller words. Consider these different ways of defining a variable

- **donateheretoday** – hard to read – are you saying "Donate Here Today" or "Don Ate Here Today"?
- **donate_here_today** – (Snake Case) Better because the underscore

separates the words

- **donateHereToday** – (Camel Case) First word is lower case, other words are capitalized. One can see the different words.

- **DonateHereToday** – (Pascal Case) First letter of every word is capitalized.

We will discuss which types are typically used with different types in a different section. For now, let us discuss different data types supported in Python.

Python Variables

Programs require data that changes while the program executes. For example an accounting program will add up all the transactions to find the total and as each transaction is added, the total is changing. Variables are used to store values and can be updated during program execution. Unlike other related language programming software, Python doesn't require declaring a variable as a single type and the variable type can change after being set. Python values are initially undefined like in most other programming languages.

Variables in Python are described as memory reserved for storing data values. Python variables act as storage units that feed the necessary data to the computer for processing.

Each variable is categorized as a number, string, tuple, dictionary, or list, among others. As you create programs, you will start to understand how variables work and how fundamental they are in creating effective Python programs. This section introduces variables but as you work through this book, you will learn how programmers declare and manipulate variables.

Variable vs. Constants

Variables and constants are two components used in Python programming but perform separate functions. Variables, as well as constants, utilize values used to create codes to execute during program creation.

As the names imply, variables are storage locations for data in the memory that can change while constants are special variables whose value never changes.

By convention, variables are written as lower case words or snake case while constants are declared with capital letters separated by underscores.

> *some_simple_name = "simple name"*
> *MY_PI_CONST = 3.1415*

Naming Variables

The naming of variables is straightforward once you know the rules. Consistency, style, and adhering to variable naming conventions ensure that your code is readable and maintainable both today and in the future.

The rules are:

- Names must have a single word, that is, with no spaces.
- Names must only comprise of letters and numbers as well as underscores such as (_).
- The first letter must never be a number.
- Reserved words must never be used as variable names.

When naming variables, remember that Python is case-sensitive so avoid creating the same names within a single program.

The Python community has created a style guide and best practices document named PEP8.

Convention for naming variables is to name the variable using snake case.

When creating variable names, make the name descriptive so that when you return to the program at a later time, it is obvious from the name what the variable is used for. A more descriptive name is also preferred among other programmers in your team.

Python Numbers

These data types store numbers. The age of a student is an example. Consider the example given below:

total = 55
age = 26

The numbers are being assigned to the variables 'total' and 'age'.

Variables can also be deleted. The 'del' statement can be used for the deletion of single or multiple variables. This is shown below:

del total
del total, age

In the first statement, we are deleting a single variable, while in the second statement, we are deleting two variables. If the variables to be deleted are two or more, separate them with a comma.

In Python, there are three numerical values that are supported:
- Integer (int)
- Whole numbers such as when counting. (ie. 1, 2, 3)
- Floating Point (float)

Python Programming

- Decimal numbers (ie. pi = 3.1415)
- Complex (complex)
- Special numbers with a real and imaginary part. (ie pythag = 3 + 4j)

In Python 3, all integers are represented in the form of long integers.

The Python integer literals belong to the int class.

Integer Example

Run the following statements consecutively on the Python interactive interpreter:

```
>>> x = 10
>>> x
10
>>>
```

Float Example

Let's see how the float is used for storing numeric values with a decimal point.

```
>>> x=10.345
>>> x
10.345
>>>
```

Float and Integer Example

If you are performing an operation with one of the operands being a float and the other being an integer, the result will be a float.

```
>>> 5 * 1.5
7.5
>>>
```

As shown above, the result of the operation is 7.5, which is a float.

Complex Number Example

Complex numbers are made of real and imaginary parts, with the imaginary part being denoted using a j. They can be defined as follows:

```
>>> x = 4 + 5j
>>> x
(4+5j)
>>>
```

In the above example, 4 is the real part, while 5 is the imaginary part.

Python Strings

- Python strings are a series of characters enclosed within quotes. Use any type of quotes to enclose Python strings, that is, either single or double quotes.

- String characters begin at index 0, meaning that the first character string is at index 0. This is good when you need to access string characters.

- To concatenate strings in Python, we use + operator; the asterisk (*) is used for repetition.

- To access elements in the string, we use the slice operator.

String Example

```
#!/usr/bin/python3

thanks = 'Thank You'
print (thanks) # to print the complete string
print (thanks[0]) # to print the first character of the string
print (thanks[2:7]) # to print the 3rd to the 7th character of the string
print (thanks[4:]) # to print from the 5th character of the string
print (thanks * 2) # to print the string two times
print (thanks + "\tAgain!") # to print a concatenated string
```

The program prints the following once executed:

```
Thank You
T
ank Y
k You
Thank YouThank You
Thank You  Again
```

Let's recap this program with strings.

We defined a string named thanks with the value "Thank You".

The **print (thanks[0])** statement helps us access the first character of the string; hence it prints 'T'.

You also notice that the space between the two words is counted as a character.

Notice that we have text that begins with the '#' symbol. The '#' symbol is the beginning of a comment. The Python print will ignore the text starting from the '#' symbol until to the end of the line.

Comments are meant to enhance the readability of code by giving explanations.

Python Boolean

A Python boolean type has a value of either **True** or **False**. The use of boolean values is described in more detail in the Python Comparisons section below but a short overview is useful for understanding this type.

Booleans are useful when checking a condition. Conditions are used when making a decision. If something is "true" then do something, otherwise do something else. We'll dig into conditionals more later.

Python Collections

A Python variable typically refers to a single storage element.

A Collection typically refers to multiple variables grouped together. Collections are used a lot in Python and is one of the primary reasons Python is so popular in Data Science.

The following sections will give a brief description of common Python Collection Types which include **Lists**, **Tuples**, **Sets**, and **Dictionaries**. These collection types are discussed in more detail after the brief introduction of each type.

Python Lists

Python lists offer changeable and ordered data and can be recognized by their square brackets enclosing one or more elements, for example, ["apple", "cherry"].

- Elements of the Python list can be changed.
- Elements of the Python list will keep the order they are created and updated to. In other words, the value at index 0 will not change unless you change it.
- Similar to Python strings, you can access an existing list by referring to the

index number.

- Reference elements from the end of the list using negative indexes such as '-1' or '-2'.
- You can extract a subset from a list using the start and end indexes.
- Since items in a list can be modified, select the item to be modified using the index (starting index is 0) of the item.
- Loop through items on the list
- Add or remove items to a list
- Confirm if items are available in the list.

Let's use different flying birds as an example. We could create a separate variable for each bird to hold their name

```
#!/usr/bin/python3

bird1_name = "Vulture"
bird2_name = "Swan"
bird3_name = "Crane"
```

but it would be better to use a list to hold all the birds names together since it is a group.#!/usr/bin/python3

```
flying_birds = ["Vulture", "Swan", "Crane", "Goose", "Mallard", "Stork"]
```

Every item belonging to a list corresponds to an index numerical value, which is an integer starting from 0 as I mentioned above.

For our list flying_birds, the indexing is as follows:

'Vulture'	'Swan'	'Crane'	'Goose'	'Mallard'	'Stork'
0	1	2	3	4	5

From the above items, the first item 'Vulture' takes the position of index zero (0), and the list comes to an end at index 5 which is 'Stork'.

In Python, each item comes with a specific index number attached to it. This means we can call a specific item individually through its index syntax enabling us to manipulate it as we wish without affecting other items. This is also the same way other sequential data types function.

Python Tuples

Python Tuples are similar to Python Lists but cannot be changed. Tuples offer ordered data and are recognized by their brackets enclosing one or more elements, for example, ("apple", "cherry"). Tuples have the following characteristics in common with Lists:

- Elements of the Python tuple will keep the order they are created and updated to. In other words, the value at index 0 will not change unless you change it.

- Similar to Python strings, you can access an existing tuple element by referring to the index number.

- Reference elements from the end of the tuple using negative indexes such as '-1' or '-2'.

- You can extract a subset from a tuple using the start and end indexes.

- Loop through items in the tuple

- Confirm if items are available in the tuple.

The major difference between Lists and Tuples?

- Tuples do not allow elements to be modified, added or removed like lists.

Python Sets

Python sets are recognized by the curly brackets enclosing one or more elements, for example, {"apple", "cherry"}.

Python Sets are similar to Python Lists with more limitations such as:

- Cannot be changed, added or removed.
- Are not ordered (cannot access element by index because the set can change)
- Duplicate elements are not allowed.

Python Dictionaries

Python dictionaries are used to store data in "key":"value" pairs. Dictionaries can be recognized by the curly brackets enclosing these key-value pairs.

An example of a dictionary would be:

```
{
"fruit_name": "apple",
"fruit_price": 3.25,
"fruit_qty": 12
}
```

Which is a grouping that could be used by a grocery store to indicate "buying 12 apples has a cost of $3.25".

Notice how the key defines the value and the value can be a string, an integer or a float.

Determining Type

In Python, there is a method named **type()** that can be used for determining the type of a variable. You only have to pass the name of the variable inside that function as the argument, and its type will be printed.

```
>>> x=10
>>> type(x)
<class 'int'>
>>>
```

The variable x is of class int, as shown above.

You can try it for other variable types, as shown below:

```
>>> name='nicholas'
>>> type(name)
<class 'string'>
>>>
```

This shows that the variable name is of the string class.

Digging Deeper Into Python Strings

Strings are possibly the most significant information type since they are utilized in essentially every situation. We need strings to interact with the user as alerts, prompts, declarations, and other results that can be read by people.

There will be times where you need to manipulate strings. Maybe you'll need to get its length, or you'll need to split it apart into sub-strings or make another string from it. Maybe you'll need to read what character is at x position. Whatever the reason, the point is that there are ways to manipulate strings in Python.

Python Programming

Go ahead and create a new file. As always, you can call it whatever you want. My file is going to be named strings.py. Uncreative name, sure, but we're going to be getting creative with strings, believe me.

So what is a string, really? We obviously know that a string is a line of text. But what goes into that?

We introduces lists earlier. Lists are actually a form of another variable that's called "array" in other languages but called a list in Python. A list (or array) is a pre-allocated group of data that goes together.

Words are created from letters of the alphabet. In programming, letters are also referred to as characters (commonly shorted to "char"). When grouped together, these letters combine to become a word. A string is one or more words so it is a collection of characters.

In terms of computer-speak; there isn't native support for strings. Strings were simply arrays of characters. For example, if one wanted to make a string called "hello," they would have done the following in other programming languages:

char hello[6] = { 'h', 'e', 'l', 'l', 'o', '\0'};

Python, in its beautiful habit of maximum abstraction, hides these complexities and lets us just declare:

hello = "hello"

The point is that strings, ultimately, are just sets of data. And like any set of data, they can be manipulated. There will be times, too, where we need to manipulate them.

The most simple form of string manipulation is the concept of concatenation or combining two or more strings. Concatenated strings are strings that are put together to form a new string. Concatenation is super easy—you simply use the + sign to add the strings together.

> *#!/usr/bin/python3*
>
> *sentence = "My" + "grandmother" + "baked" + "today."*
> *print(sentence)*

> *# would print "Mygrandmotherbakedtoday."*

> Which is probably not what we want. We want spaces in between so there are 2 ways to do this. Either add the spaces in the strings or concatenate with spaces.*#!/usr/bin/python3*
>
> *sentence = "My " + "grandmother " + "baked " + "today."*
> *print(sentence)*

> Note the space after "My ", "grandmother " and "baked " which gives:"My grandmother baked today."

Ahh. Much better!

The first thing to remember when working with string manipulation is that strings, like any set of data, start counting at 0. So the string "backpack" would count like so:

b	a	c	k	p	a	c	k
0	1	2	3	4	5	6	7
-8	-7	-6	-5	-4	-3	-2	-1

There are a few different things that we can do with this knowledge alone. The first is that we can extract a single letter from it.

Let's say that the string "backpack" was stored in a variable called a backpack.

> *backpack = "backpack"*

> We could extract the letter "p" from it by writing:letter = backpack[4]

This would extract the character at index 4 in the string and store it in the variable letter. Here, of course, it's 'p'.

> If we wanted to extract the characters from "b" to "p," we could do the following: short_string = backpack[0 : 5]

This would give the variable **short_string** a string equal to the value of backpack's 0 index to 4 index but not including index 5.

short_string, thus, would have the value of **"backp"**.

There are a few more things you can do with data sets and strings in order to get more specific results.

If the first index isn't given, Python assumes the start index (index = 0). Similarly, if the last index isn't given, Python assumes the end index (last character).

Negative indexes start counting from the end.

- backpack[:4] would give you all characters from the start to index 3, like just before.
- backpack[4:] would give you all characters from index 4 to the end. **Notice that this does include the last index item.**
- backpack[-2:] would give you the last two characters.
- backpack[2:] would give you everything but the first two characters
- backpack[:-2] would give you everything aside from the last two characters.

Python String Methods

Python has even more powerful string manipulations that goes beyond this simple kind of arithmetic.

The String class has built-in functions called **methods**. Most things in Python - or object-oriented languages in general, are forms of things called objects. These are essentially variable types that have entire sets of properties associated with them.

Every single string is an instance of the "**string**" class, thus making it a string object. The string class contains definitions for methods that every string object can access as an instance of the string class.

For example, let's create a bit of a heftier string.

> *tongue_twister = "Peter Piper picked a peck of pickled peppers"*

The string class has a variety of built-in methods you can utilize in order to work with its objects.

Splitting a String Apart

Let's take the **split()** method. Here is an example using split().

```
$ python3

>>> tongue_twister = "Peter Piper picked a peck of pickled peppers"
>>> split_list = tongue_twister.split(" ")
>>> split_list
['Peter', 'Piper', 'picked', 'a', 'peck', 'of', 'pickled', 'peppers']
>>>
```

This method would split the string at every space (notice the parameter inside the split() is a space or ' ' character), giving you a list of each word in the sentence.

Printing split_list[1] would give you the value 'Piper' – the second word in the list because index 0 is the first word in the list.

Counting Characters in a String

There's also the **count()** method, which would count the number of a certain character.

```
$ python3

>>> tongue_twister = "Peter Piper picked a peck of pickled peppers"
>>> p_count1 = tongue_twister.count('p')
>>> p_count1
7
>>>
```

You would get the number 7 because there are 7 lowercase 'p' and 2 uppercase 'P'.

There are 2 'P' in the variable which don't match. Not to worry, there is another method named lower() that converts the entire string to lowercase.

```
$ python3

>>> tongue_twister = "Peter Piper picked a peck of pickled peppers"
>>> p_count2 = tongue_twister.lower().count('p')
>>> p_count2
9
>>>
```

You would get the number 9 because the variable is first converted to lowercase and then the 'p' are counted.

Replace Part of a String

There's the **replace()** method, which will replace a given string with another. For example, if you wanted to replace "peppers" with "potatoes":

```
#!/usr/bin/python3

>>> tongue_twister = "Peter Piper picked a peck of pickled peppers"
>>> tongue_twister2 = tongue_twister.replace("peppers", "potatoes")
>>> tongue_twister2
'Peter Piper picked a peck of pickled potatoes'
>>>
```

Removing White Space From Begin/End of String

There's the **strip()** method, which removes either a given character (specified inside the parenthesis) or whitespace off both sides of the string. The **lstrip()**, and **rstrip()** methods are similar but only remove from the left (**lstrip**) or right(**rstrip**) of the string. This is really useful when you're trying to parse user input. Unstripped user input can lead to unnecessarily large data sets and even buggy code.

Joining Strings

The last major one is the **join()** method, which will put a certain character between every character in the string.

```
$ python3

>>> tongue_twister = "Peter Piper picked a peck of pickled peppers"
>>> join_dash = '-'.join(tongue_twister)
>>> join_dash
'P-e-t-e-r- -P-i-p-e-r- -p-i-c-k-e-d- -a- -p-e-c-k- -o-f- -p-i-c-k-l-e-d- -p-e-p-p-e-r-s'
>>>
```

An even better use of this method is for creating a string with spaces from a list or tuple of individual words (think of this as the opposite of the split() method).

```
$ python3
>>> my_words = ["These", "words", "can", "be", "stitched", "back", "together"]
>>> my_sentence = " ".join(my_words)
>>> my_sentence
'These words can be stitched back together'
>>>
```

String Tests

There are also various boolean expression methods that will return **True** or **False**.

Starts With & Ends With Test

The **startswith**(character) and **endswith**(character) methods are two fantastic examples and can be used like this:

```
$ python3

>>> tongue_twister = "Peter Piper picked a peck of pickled peppers"
>>> starts_with_p = tongue_twister.startswith('P')
>>> starts_with_p
True
>>> starts_with_h = tongue_twister.startswith('H')
>>> starts_with_h
False
>>>
```

The **endswith()** method works in a similar fashion.

These are used for an internal evaluation of strings as well as for evaluating user input.

Other String Tests

A few other examples are

- **isalnum**() that will see if all characters in the string are alphanumeric or if there are special characters,
- **isalpha**() that will see if all characters in the string are alphabetic,
- **isdigit**() which will check to see if the string is a digit or not, and
- **isspace**() which will check to see if the string is a space or not.

These are all extremely useful for parsing a given string and deciding what to do if the string is or isn't a certain way.

More information about what String Functions are available and how they can be used can be found on the web at docs.python.org/3/library/string.html (search for Python string functions).

Digging Deeper Into Python Booleans

When developing a software program, there is often a need to confirm and verify whether an expression is true or false. This is where Python Boolean data type and data values are used. In Python, comparison and evaluation of two data values will result in one of the two Boolean values: "**True**" or "**False**."

Here are some examples of the comparison statement of numeric data leading to

Boolean value:

> *print (100 > 90)*
> *OUTPUT – True*
> *print (100 == 90)*
> *OUTPUT – False*
> *print (100 < 90)*
> *OUTPUT – False*

Let's look at the "bool ()" function now, which allows for the evaluation of numeric data as well as string data resulting in "True" or "False" Boolean values.

> *print (bool (99))*
> *OUTPUT - True*
> *print (bool ("Welcome"))*
> *OUTPUT - True*

Here are some key points to remember for Booleans:

- If a statement has some kind of content, it would be evaluated as "True."

- All string data values will be evaluated as "True" unless the string is empty.

- All numeric values will be evaluated as "True" except "0."

- Lists, Tuples, Set, and Dictionaries will be evaluated as "True" unless they are empty.

- Mostly empty values like (), [], {}, "", False, None and 0 will be evaluated as "False."

- Any object created with the "len" function that results in the data value as "0" or "False" will be evaluated as "False."

> In Python, there are various built-in functions function that can be evaluated as Boolean, for example, the "**isinstance()**" function, which allows you to determine the data type of an object. Therefore, in order to check if an object is an integer, the code will be as below: X = 123
>
> *print (isinstance (X, int))*

Exercise

Create two variables, "X" with string data values as "Just do it!" and "Y" with numeric data value as "3.24" and evaluate them.

Try it before looking at the answer - Write Your Code First

Now, check your code against the correct code below:

X = "Just do it!"
Y = 3.24
Z = None
print (bool (X))
print (bool (Y))
print(bool (Z))

OUTPUT –
True
True
False

Digging Deeper into Python Lists

In Python, lists are collections of data types that can be changed, organized, and may include duplicate values.

Creating a List

Lists are written within square brackets, as shown in the syntax below.

```
$ python3

>>> X = ["string001", "string002", "string003"]
>>> print (X)
['string001', 'string002', 'string003']
>>>
```

You can also use the "**list ( )**" constructor to create a List, as shown in the example below: $ python3

```
>>> List = list(["string001", "string002", "string003"])
>>> print(List)
['string001', 'string002', 'string003']
>>>
```

The same concept of position applies to the **Lists** as the **String** data type, which dictates that the first string is at position 0. Subsequently, the strings that will follow are given positions 1, 2, and so on.

Element at Index

You can selectively display the desired string from a List by referencing the position of that string inside the square bracket in the print command, as shown below.

```
$ python3

>>> X = ["string001", "string002", "string003"]
>>> print (X[2])
string003
>>>
```

Element at Negative Index

Similarly, the concept of negative indexing is also applied to Python List. Let's look at the example below:

Element	String001	string002	string003
Index	0	1	2
Negative Index	-3	-2	-1

```
$ python3

>>> X = ["string001", "string002", "string003"]
>>> print (X[-2])
string002
>>>
```

Extracting Part of a List

You will also be able to specify a range of indexes by indicating the start and end of a range. The result in values of such command on a Python List would be a new List containing only the indicated items. Here is an example for your reference.

```
$ python3

>>> X = ["string001", "string002", "string003", "string004", "string005", "string006"]
>>> print (X[2:4])
['string003', 'string004']
>>>
```

Remember, the first item is at position 0, and the final position of the range (4) is not included.

Extracting the First Elements of a List

Now, if you do not indicate the start of this range, it will default to the position 0, as shown in the example below:

```
$ python3

>>> X = ["string001", "string002", "string003", "string004"]
>>> print (X[:3])
['string001', 'string002', 'string003']
>>>
```

Extracting the Last Elements of a List

Similarly, if you do not indicate the end of this range, it will display all the items of the List from the indicated start range to the end of the List, as shown in the example below:

```
$ python3

>>> X = ["string001", "string002", "string003", "string004", "string005", "string006"]
>>> print (X[3:])
['string004', 'string005', 'string006']
>>>
```

You can also specify a range of negative indexes to Python Lists, as shown in the example below:

```
$ python3

>>> X = ["string001", "string002", "string003", "string004", "string005", "string006"]
>>> print (X[-3:-1])
['string004', 'string005']
>>>
```

Remember, the last item is at position -1, and the final position of this range (-1) is not included in the Output.

Changing Element in a List

There might be instances when you need to change the data value for a Python List. This can be accomplished by referring to the index number of that item and declaring the new value. Let's look at the example below:

```
$ python3

>>> X = ["string001", "string002", "string003", "string004", "string005", "string006"]
>>> X [3] = "newstring"
>>> print (X)
['string001', 'string002', 'string003', 'newstring', 'string005', 'string006']
>>>
```

You can also add a new item to an existing Python List at a specific position using the built-in "**insert ()**" method, as shown in the example below:

```
$ python3

>>> X = ["string001", "string002", "string003", "string004"]
>>> print (X)
['string001', 'string002', 'string003', 'string004']
>>> X.insert(2, "newstring")
>>> print (X)
['string001', 'string002', 'newstring', 'string003', 'string004']
>>>
```

Notice that this actually added "newstring" to the list and the list now has 5 elements.

Determining Length of a List

You can also determine the length of a Python List using the "**len()**" function, as shown in the example below:

```
$ python3

>>> X = ["string001", "string002", "string003", "string004", "string005", "string006"]
>>> print (len (X))
6
>>>
```

Appending to a List

Python Lists can also be changed by adding new items to an existing list using the built-in "**append ()**" method, as shown in the example below:

```
$ python3

>>> X = ["string001", "string002", "string003", "string004"]
>>> print (X)
['string001', 'string002', 'string003', 'string004']
>>> X.append("newstring")
>>> print (X)
['string001', 'string002', 'string003', 'string004', 'newstring']
>>>
```

Copying Existing Python List

There might be instances when you need to copy an existing Python List. This can be accomplished by using the built-in "**copy ()**" method or the "**list ()**" method, as shown in the example below:

```
$ python3

>>> X = ["string001", "string002", "string003", "string004", "string005", "string006"]
>>> Y = X.copy()
>>> print(Y)
['string001', 'string002', 'string003', 'string004', 'string005', 'string006']
>>>
>>> Z = list(X)
>>> print(Z)
['string001', 'string002', 'string003', 'string004', 'string005', 'string006']
>>>
```

Deleting Element from List

There are multiple built-in methods to delete items from a Python List.

To delete a specific item selectively, the "remove ()" method can be used.

```
$ python3

>>> X = ["string001", "string002", "string003", "string004"]
>>> X.remove ("string002")
>>> print(X)
['string001', 'string003', 'string004']
>>>
```

To delete a specific item using the index from the List, the "**pop ()**" method can be used with the position of the value. If no index has been indicated, the last item of the index will be removed. If the result of the pop() operation is saved in a variable, that variable will hold the removed value.

```
$ python3

>>> X = ["string001", "string002", "string003", "string004"]
>>> print(X)
['string001', 'string002', 'string003', 'string004']
>>> X.pop()
'string004'
>>> print(X)
['string001', 'string002', 'string003']
>>>
```

To delete a specific index from the List, the "**del ()**" method can be used, followed by the index within square brackets.

```
$ python3

>>> X = ["string001", "string002", "string003", "string004"]
>>> print(X)
['string001', 'string002', 'string003', 'string004']
>>> del X[2]
>>> print(X)
['string001', 'string002', 'string004']
>>>
```

To delete the entire List variable, the "**del ()**" method can be used on the entire List, as shown below.

```
$ python3

>>> X = ["string001", "string002", "string003", "string004"]
>>> del X
>>> print(X)
Traceback (most recent call last):
  File "<stdin>", line 1, in <module>
NameError: name 'X' is not defined
>>>
```

To delete all the string values from the List without deleting the variable itself, the "**clear ()**" method can be used, as shown below.

Python Programming

```
$ python3

>>> X = ["string001", "string002", "string003", "string004"]
>>> print(X)
['string001', 'string002', 'string003', 'string004']
>>> X.clear()
>>> print(X)
[]
>>>
```

Concatenation of Lists

You can join multiple lists with the use of the "+" logical operator

```
$ python3

>>> X = ["string001", "string002", "string003", "string004"]
>>> Y = [10, 20, 30, 40]
>>> Z = X + Y
>>> print(Z)
['string001', 'string002', 'string003', 'string004', 10, 20, 30, 40]
>>>
```

*or by adding all the items from one list to another using the "**append ( )**" method.*

```
$ python3

>>> X = ["string001", "string002", "string003", "string004"]
>>> Y = [10, 20, 30, 40]
>>> X.append(Y)
>>> print(X)
['string001', 'string002', 'string003', 'string004', [10, 20, 30, 40]]
>>>
>>> print(X[-1])
[10, 20, 30, 40]
>>>
```

Note that the entire array of Y has been added as a single element which is different than we saw with the "**+**" operator.

The "**extend ( )**" method can be used to add a list at the end of another list. Let's look at the examples below to understand these commands.

```
$ python3

>>> X = ["string001", "string002", "string003", "string004"]
>>> Y = [10, 20, 30, 40]
>>> X.extend(Y)
>>> print(X)
['string001', 'string002', 'string003', 'string004', 10, 20, 30, 40]
>>> print(Y)
[10, 20, 30, 40]
>>>
```

List Exercises

Exercise – Create a list "A" with string data values as "red, olive, cyan, lilac, mustard" and display the item that is 2nd from the end.

Before Looking at the Answer Below, Try Writing Your Code First

Now, check your code against the correct code below:

```
$ python3

>>> A = ["red", "olive", "cyan", "lilac", "mustard"]
>>> print(A[-2])
lilac
>>>
```

Exercise – Create a list "A" with string data values as "red, olive, cyan, lilac, mustard" and display the items ranging from the string on the second position to the end of the string.

Before Looking at the Answer Below, Try Writing Your Code First

Now, check your code against the correct code below:

```
$ python3

>>> A = ["red", "olive", "cyan", "lilac", "mustard"]
>>> print(A[2:])
['cyan', 'lilac', 'mustard']
>>>
```

Exercise – Create a list "A" with string data values as "red, olive, cyan, lilac, mustard" and replace the string "olive" with "teal."

Before Looking at the Answer Below, Try Writing Your Code First

Now, check your code against the correct code below:

```
$ python3

>>> A = ["red", "olive", "cyan", "lilac", "mustard"]
>>> A[1] = "teal"
>>> print(A)
['red', 'teal', 'cyan', 'lilac', 'mustard']
>>>
```

Exercise – Create a list "A" with string data values as "red, olive, cyan, lilac, mustard" and copy the list "A" to create list "B."

Before Looking at the Answer Below, Try Writing Your Code First

Now, check your code against the correct code below:

```
$ python3

>>> A = ["red", "olive", "cyan", "lilac", "mustard"]
>>> B = A.copy()
>>> print(A)
['red', 'olive', 'cyan', 'lilac', 'mustard']
>>> print(B)
['red', 'olive', 'cyan', 'lilac', 'mustard']
>>>
```

Exercise – Create a list "A" with string data values as "red, olive, cyan, lilac, mustard" and delete the strings "red" and "lilac."

Before Looking at the Answer Below, Try Writing Your Code First

Now, check your code against the correct code below:

```
$ python3

>>> A = ["red", "olive", "cyan", "lilac", "mustard"]
>>> A.remove("red")
>>> A.remove("lilac")
>>> print(A)
['olive', 'cyan', 'mustard']
>>>
```

How to Organize a List

Sorting your list would be handy in Python, right? This section focuses on organizing lists. Python uses the list. **sort ()** method that enables you to organize your list in different ways such as in:

- Ascending order.
- Descending order.

You can also use a built-in method **sorted ()** that generates a sorted list from any iterable. Most Python beginners have difficulty deciding which method to use for sorting. ***You are advised to mostly use the list. sort () method because of various reasons***:

- List.sort () method is much faster than the sorted() method. It loads the list first followed by the method that calls the function without any arguments as compared to the sorted () method that calls the functions using the list as the argument.

- List.sort () method works with the list in place, and therefore, does not have to make a copy of the list. Contrarily, the sorted () method has to make copies of the list and works with any iterable. This makes a list. sort () method more efficient.

Both the list. **sort ()** method and **sorted ()** methods organize the lists in ascending order by default. This section guides you on the various ways of how to organize lists containing numbers, strings, tuples, and also objects.

Sorting Number Lists

Sorting number lists in Python is the easiest sort to understand. Below is an example provided on how to organize your numerical list. *L* will be used to represent the name of the list.

Ascending Order with sort()

```
$ python3

>>> L = [67, 3, 16, 74, 2]
>>> print(L)
[67, 3, 16, 74, 2]
>>> L.sort()
>>> print(L)
[2, 3, 16, 67, 74]
>>>
```

Descending order with sort()

Python Programming

```
$ python3

>>> L = [67, 3, 16, 74, 2]
>>> print(L)
[67, 3, 16, 74, 2]
>>> L.sort(reverse=True)
>>> print(L)
[74, 67, 16, 3, 2]
>>>
```

If you want to implement using the **sorted ()** method, here is how to do it:

Ascending Order with sorted()

```
$ python3
>>> L = [67, 3, 16, 74, 2]
>>> print(L)
[67, 3, 16, 74, 2]
>>> sorted_list = sorted(L)
>>> print(L)
[67, 3, 16, 74, 2]
>>> print(sorted_list)
[2, 3, 16, 67, 74]
>>>
```

Descending order with sorted()

```
$ python3

>>> L = [67, 3, 16, 74, 2]
>>> print(L)
[67, 3, 16, 74, 2]
>>> sorted_list = sorted(L, reverse=True)
>>> print(L)
[67, 3, 16, 74, 2]
>>> print(sorted_list)
[74, 67, 16, 3, 2]
>>>
```

The **sorted()** method does not require definition since it is a built-in function found on every Python installation.

It does not contain any additional arguments because it is organizing the values in L from the smallest to the largest by default.

This method does not change the original values of *L* in place.

Sorting String Lists

A string is a set of characters. In a scenario where you are provided with strings and not numbers, the list will be sorted in alphabetical order (a then b then c ...).

Ascending Order with sort()

Python Programming

```
$ python3

>>> F = ["guava", "mango", "pineapple", "avocado"]
>>> print(F)
['guava', 'mango', 'pineapple', 'avocado']
>>> F.sort()
>>> print(F)
['avocado', 'guava', 'mango', 'pineapple']
>>>
```

Descending order with sort()

```
$ python3

>>> F = ["guava", "mango", "pineapple", "avocado"]
>>> print(F)
['guava', 'mango', 'pineapple', 'avocado']
>>> F.sort(reverse=True)
>>> print(F)
['pineapple', 'mango', 'guava', 'avocado']
>>>
```

If you want to implement using the **sorted ()** method, here is how to do it:

Ascending Order with sorted()

```
$ python3
>>> F = ["guava", "mango", "pineapple", "avocado"]
>>> print(F)
['guava', 'mango', 'pineapple', 'avocado']
>>> sorted_fruit = sorted(F)
>>> print(F)
['guava', 'mango', 'pineapple', 'avocado']
>>> print(sorted_fruit)
['avocado', 'guava', 'mango', 'pineapple']
>>>
```

Descending order with sorted()

```
$ python3

>>> F = ["guava", "mango", "pineapple", "avocado"]
>>> print(F)
['guava', 'mango', 'pineapple', 'avocado']
>>> sorted_fruit = sorted(F, reverse=True)
>>> print(F)
['guava', 'mango', 'pineapple', 'avocado']
>>> print(sorted_fruit)
['pineapple', 'mango', 'guava', 'avocado']
>>>
```

In a different scenario where your list of strings is composed of both uppercase and lowercase strings, the output will differ from the rest mentioned above. Uppercase strings in Python are normally treated as "lower" characters than the lowercase strings. Here is an example that will help you understand better.

Uppercase vs Lowercase Sorting

```
$ python3

>>> R = ["town", "country", "Kenya", "home"]
>>> print(R)
['town', 'country', 'Kenya', 'home']
>>> R.sort()
>>> print(R)
['Kenya', 'country', 'home', 'town']
>>>
```

Case Insensitive Sorting

Case insensitive sorting can be done through the use of a certain parameter referred to as *key* which is utilized by both the sort and the sorted method. It assists in specifying the function to be called from the items in a list. Take a close look at the example below.

```
$ python3

>>> R = ["town", "country", "Kenya", "home"]
>>> print(R)
['town', 'country', 'Kenya', 'home']
>>> R.sort(key=str.lower)
>>> print(R)
['country', 'home', 'Kenya', 'town']
>>>
```

The **str.lower** has instructed the sort method to perform the sorting on all the lowercase strings. The parameter has enabled you to change the default behavior.

Digging Deeper into Python Tuples

In Python, Tuples are collections of data types that cannot be changed but can be arranged in a specific order.

Creating a Tuple

You can create a **Tuple** directly by enclosing the elements in ()

```
$ python3

>>> Tuple1 = ("string01", "string02", "string03", "string04")
>>> print(Tuple1)
('string01', 'string02', 'string03', 'string04')
>>>
```

You can also use the "**tuple ( )**" constructor to create a **Tuple**, as shown in the example below:

```
$ python3

>>> Tuple1 = tuple(("string01", "string02", "string03", "string04"))
>>> print(Tuple1)
('string01', 'string02', 'string03', 'string04')
>>>
```

Extracting an Element from a Tuple

Similar to the Python **List**, you can selectively display the desired string from a **Tuple** by referencing the position of that string inside the square bracket in the print command as shown below.

```
$ python3

>>> Tuple = ("string01", "string02", "string03")
>>> print(Tuple[1])
string02
>>>
```

Extracting an Element from the End of a Tuple

The concept of negative indexing can also be applied to Python **Tuple**, as shown in the example below:

```
$ python3

>>> Tuple = ("string01", "string02", "string03", "string04", "string05")
>>> print(Tuple[-2])
string04
>>>
```

Extracting Elements from a Tuple

You will also be able to specify a range of indexes by indicating the start and end of a range. The result in values of such command on a Python **Tuple** would be a new Tuple containing only the indicated items, as shown in the example below:

```
$ python3

>>> Tuple = ("string01", "string02", "string03", "string04", "string05", "string06")
>>> print(Tuple[1:5])
('string02', 'string03', 'string04', 'string05')
>>>
```

Remember, the first item is at position 0, and the final position of the range, which is the fifth position in this example, is not included.

Extracting Elements from the End of a Tuple

You can also specify a range of negative indexes to Python **Tuples**, as shown in the example below:

```
$ python3

>>> Tuple = ("string01", "string02", "string03", "string04", "string05", "string06")
>>> print(Tuple[-4:-2])
('string03', 'string04')
>>>
```

Remember, the last item is at position **-1**, and the final position of this range, which is the -2 position in this example, is not included in the Output.

Workaround for Modifying Tuple

Unlike Python **Lists**, you cannot directly change the data value of Python **Tuples** after they have been created. However, conversion of a Tuple into a List and then modifying the data value of that List will allow you to create a Tuple subsequently from that updated List. Let's look at the example below:

```
$ python3

>>> Tuple1 = ("string01", "string02", "string03", "string04", "string05", "string06")
>>> print(Tuple1)
('string01', 'string02', 'string03', 'string04', 'string05', 'string06')
>>> List1 = list(Tuple1)
>>> List1[2] = "Update List & Create New Tuple"
>>> Tuple1 = tuple(List1)
>>> print(Tuple1)
('string01', 'string02', 'Update List & Create New Tuple', 'string04', 'string05', 'string06')
>>>
```

Length of a Tuple

You can also determine the length of a Python Tuple using the "**len()**" function, as shown in the example below:

```
$ python3

>>> Tuple = ("string01", "string02", "string03", "string04", "string05", "string06")
>>> print(len(Tuple))
6
>>>
```

Deletion Rules of a Tuple

You cannot selectively delete items from a Tuple, but you can use the "**del**" keyword to delete the Tuple in its entirety, as shown in the example below:

```
$ python3

>>> Tuple = ("string01", "string02", "string03", "string04", "string05", "string06")
>>> print(Tuple)
('string01', 'string02', 'string03', 'string04', 'string05', 'string06')
>>> del Tuple
>>> print(Tuple)
Traceback (most recent call last):
  File "<stdin>", line 1, in <module>
NameError: name 'Tuple' is not defined
>>>
```

Joining Tuples

You can join multiple Tuples with the use of the "**+**" logical operator.

```
$ python3

>>> Tuple1 = ("string01", "string02", "string03", "string04")
>>> Tuple2 = (100, 200, 300)
>>> Tuple3 = Tuple1 + Tuple2
>>> print(Tuple3)
('string01', 'string02', 'string03', 'string04', 100, 200, 300)
>>>
```

Tuple Exercises

Exercise – Create a Tuple "X" with string data values as "pies, cake, bread, scone, cookies" and display the item at -3 position.

Before Looking at the Answer Below, Try Writing Your Code First

Now, check your code against the correct code below:

```
$ python3

>>> X = ("pies", "cake", "bread", "scone", "cookies")
>>> print(X[-3])
bread
>>>
```

Exercise – Create a Tuple "X" with string data values as "pies, cake, bread, scone, cookies" and display items ranging from -4 to -2.

Before Looking at the Answer Below, Try Writing Your Code First

Now, check your code against the correct code below:

```
$ python3

>>> X = ("pies", "cake", "bread", "scone", "cookies")
>>> print(X[-4:-2])
('cake', 'bread')
>>>
```

Exercise – Create a Tuple "X" with string data values as "pies, cake, bread, scone, cookies" and change its item from "cookies" to "tart" using the List function.

Before Looking at the Answer Below, Try Writing Your Code First

Now, check your code against the code below:

```
$ python3

>>> X = ("pies", "cake", "bread", "scone", "cookies")
>>> print(X)
('pies', 'cake', 'bread', 'scone', 'cookies')
>>> List1 = list(X)
>>> List1[-1] = "tart"
>>> X = tuple(List1)
>>> print(X)
('pies', 'cake', 'bread', 'scone', 'tart')
>>>
```

Exercise – Create a Tuple "X" with string data values as "pies, cake, cookies" and another Tuple "Y" with numeric data values as (2, 12, 22), then join them together.

Before Looking at the Answer Below, Try Writing Your Code First

Now, check your code against the code below:

```
$ python3

>>> X = ("pies", "cake", "cookies")
>>> Y = (2, 12, 22)
>>> Z = X + Y
>>> print(Z)
('pies', 'cake', 'cookies', 2, 12, 22)
>>>
```

Digging Deeper into Python Sets

In Python, sets are collections of data types that cannot be organized and indexed. Sets do not allow duplicate items and must be written within curly brackets, as shown in the syntax below:

Creating a Set

You can create a set directly by enclosing the elements in {}

```
$ python3

>>> Set1 = {"set1", "set2", "set3"}
>>> print(Set1)
{'set2', 'set1', 'set3'}
>>>
```

Notice the order of strings isn't the same as we initialized with.

You can also use the "**set ()**" constructor to create a Set, as shown in the example below:

```
$ python3

>>> Set1 = set(("set1", "set2", "set3"))
>>> print(Set1)
{'set2', 'set1', 'set3'}
>>>
```

Unlike the Python **List** and **Tuple**, you cannot selectively display desired items from a **Set** by referencing the position of that item because the Python Set are not arranged in any order. Therefore, items do not have any indexing. However, the "for" loop can be used on Sets (more on this topic later in this chapter).

Unlike Python **Lists**, you cannot directly change the data values of Python **Sets** after they have been created.

Adding Elements to Set

However, you can use the "**add ()**" method to add a single item to Set and use the "**update ( )**" method to add one or more items to an already existing Set. Let's look at the example below:

```
$ python3

>>> Set1 = {"set1", "set2", "set3"}
>>> print(Set1)
{'set2', 'set1', 'set3'}
>>> Set1.add("newstring")
>>> print(Set1)
{'set2', 'set1', 'newstring', 'set3'}
>>>
```

Adding Elements to Set with Update()

You can also add with the "**update()**" function.

```
$ python3

>>> Set1 = {"set1", "set2", "set3"}
>>> print(Set1)
{'set2', 'set1', 'set3'}
>>> Set1.update(["newset1", "newset2"])
>>> print(Set1)
{'set2', 'newset1', 'set3', 'set1', 'newset2'}
>>>
```

Determining the Length of a Set

You can also determine the length of a Python Set using the "**len()**" function, as shown.

```
$ python3

>>> Set1 = {"set1", "set2", "set3"}
>>> print(len(Set1))
3
>>>
```

Selectively Delete an Element from a Set

To selectively delete a specific item from a Set, the "**remove ()**" method can be used as shown in the code below:

```
$ python3

>>> Set1 = {"set1", "set2", "set3", "set4", "set5"}
>>> print(Set1)
{'set2', 'set5', 'set3', 'set1', 'set4'}
>>> Set1.remove("set1")
>>> print(Set1)
{'set2', 'set5', 'set3', 'set4'}
>>>
```

You can also use the "**discard ( )**" method to delete specific items from a Set, as shown in the example below:

```
$ python3

>>> Set1 = {"set1", "set2", "set3", "set4", "set5"}
>>> print(Set1)
{'set2', 'set5', 'set3', 'set1', 'set4'}
>>> Set1.discard("set5")
>>> print(Set1)
{'set2', 'set3', 'set1', 'set4'}
>>>
```

The "**pop ( )**" method can be used to delete only the last item of a Set. It must be noted this is dangerous since the Python Sets are unordered, any item that the system deems as the last item will be removed. As a result, the output of this method will be the item that has been removed.

```
$ python3

>>> Set1 = {"set1", "set2", "set3", "set4", "set5"}
>>> print(Set1)
{'set2', 'set5', 'set3', 'set1', 'set4'}
>>> A = Set1.pop()
>>> print(A)
set2
>>> print(Set1)
{'set5', 'set3', 'set1', 'set4'}
>>>
```

Delete the Entire Set

To delete the entire set, the "**del**" keyword can be used, as shown below.

```
$ python3

>>> Set1 = {"set1", "set2", "set3", "set4", "set5"}
>>> print(Set1)
{'set2', 'set5', 'set3', 'set1', 'set4'}
>>> del Set1
>>> print(Set1)
Traceback (most recent call last):
  File "<stdin>", line 1, in <module>
NameError: name 'Set1' is not defined
>>>
```

Delete All the Contents of a Set

To delete all the items from the set without deleting the variable itself, the "**clear ()**" method can be used, as shown below:

```
$ python3

>>> Set1 = {"set1", "set2", "set3", "set4", "set5"}
>>> print(Set1)
{'set2', 'set5', 'set3', 'set1', 'set4'}
>>> Set1.clear()
>>> print(Set1)
set()
>>>
```

You can join multiple Sets with the use of the "**union ( )**" method. The output of this method will be a new set that contains all items from both sets.

```
$ python3

>>> Set1 = {"set1", "set2", "set3", "set4", "set5"}
>>> print(Set1)
{'set2', 'set5', 'set3', 'set1', 'set4'}
>>> Set2 = {15, 25, 35, 45, 55}
>>> print(Set2)
{35, 55, 25, 45, 15}
>>> Set3 = Set1.union(Set2)
>>> print(Set3)
{'set2', 'set5', 35, 'set3', 'set1', 45, 15, 55, 25, 'set4'}
>>>
```

You can also use the "**update ( )**" method to insert all the items from one set into another without creating a new Set.

Python Programming

```
$ python3

>>> Set1 = {"set1", "set2", "set3", "set4", "set5"}
>>> print(Set1)
{'set2', 'set5', 'set3', 'set1', 'set4'}
>>> Set2 = {15, 25, 35, 45, 55}
>>> print(Set2)
{35, 55, 25, 45, 15}
>>> Set1.update(Set2)
>>> print(Set1)
{'set2', 'set5', 35, 'set3', 'set1', 45, 15, 55, 25, 'set4'}
>>>
```

Notice how the Set doesn't have any order.

Set Exercises

Exercise – Create a Set "Veg" with string data values as "pies, cake, bread, scone, cookies" and add new items "tart," "custard," and "waffles" to this Set.

Before Looking at the Answer Below, Try Writing Your Code First

Check your code against the code below:

```
$ python3

>>> Veg = {"pies", "cake", "bread", "scone", "cookies"}
>>> print(Veg)
{'cake', 'cookies', 'scone', 'pies', 'bread'}
>>> Veg.update(["tart", "custard", "waffles"])
>>> print(Veg)
{'cake', 'cookies', 'custard', 'tart', 'waffles', 'scone', 'pies', 'bread'}
>>>
```

Exercise – Create a Set "Veg" with string data values as "pies, cake, bread, scone, cookies," then delete the last item from this Set.

Before Looking at the Answer Below, Try Writing Your Code First

Check your code against the code below:

```
$ python3

>>> Veg = {"pies", "cake", "bread", "scone", "cookies"}
>>> print(Veg)
{'cake', 'cookies', 'scone', 'pies', 'bread'}
>>> which_one = Veg.pop()
>>> print(which_one)
cake
>>> print(Veg)
{'cookies', 'scone', 'pies', 'bread'}
>>>
```

Exercise – Create a Set "Veg" with string data values as "pies, cake, bread, scone, cookies" and another Set "Veg2" with items as "tart, eggos, custard, waffles." Then combine both these Sets to create a third new Set.

Before Looking at the Answer Below, Try Writing Your Code First

Check your code against the code below:

```
$ python3

>>> Veg = {"pies", "cake", "bread", "scone", "cookies"}
>>> print(Veg)
{'cake', 'cookies', 'scone', 'pies', 'bread'}
>>> Veg2 = {"tart", "eggos", "custard", "waffles"}
>>> print(Veg2)
{'waffles', 'eggos', 'custard', 'tart'}
>>> AllVeg = Veg.union(Veg2)
>>> print(AllVeg)
{'scone', 'bread', 'cookies', 'custard', 'tart', 'waffles', 'cake', 'eggos', 'pies'}
>>>
```

Digging Deeper into Python Dictionaries

A Python **Dictionary** works in a very similar way to a regular dictionary. Python offers many different data structures to hold information, and the dictionary is one of the simplest and most useful. While many things in Python are iterables, not all of them are sequences and a Python dictionary falls in this category. In this article, we will talk about what a Python dictionary is, how it works, and what are its most common applications.

Getting clean and actionable data is one of the key challenges in data analysis. Data needs to be represented in a readable way. A Python dictionary makes it easier to read and change data, rendering it more useable for predictive modeling.

A Python dictionary is an unordered collection of data values. Unlike other data types which hold only one value as an element, a Python dictionary holds a **'key': 'value'** pair. The Python dictionary is optimized in a manner that allows it to access values when the key is known.

While each key:value pair is separated by a comma in a Python Dictionary, each key and it's corresponding value is separated by a colon. While the keys of the dictionary have to be unique and immutable, the values can be of any type and can also be repeated any number of times.

While there are several Python dictionary methods, there are some basic operations that need to be mastered. We will walk through the most important ones in this section.

Creating a Python Dictionary

To create a Python dictionary you need to put items (each having a key and a corresponding value expressed as key: value) inside curly brackets. Each item needs to be separated from the next by a comma. As discussed above, values can repeat and be of any type. Keys, on the other hand, are unique and immutable. There is also a built-in function constructor named **dict()** that you can use to create a dictionary. For easier understanding note that this built in function is written as dict() in the rest of this book.

Accessing items in the dictionary in Python is simple enough. All you need to do is put the key name of the item within square brackets. This is important because the keys are unique and non-repeatable.

Python Programming

```
$ python3

>>> my_car = {"manufacturer":"Honda", "model": "Accord", "mileage": 1245}
>>> print(my_car)
{'manufacturer': 'Honda', 'model': 'Accord', 'mileage': 1245}
>>> k = my_car["model"]
>>> print(k)
Accord
>>> print(my_car["manufacturer"])
Honda
>>>
```

You can also use another of the Python dictionary methods get() to access the item. Here's what it looks like.

```
$ python3

>>> my_car = {"manufacturer":"Honda", "model": "Accord", "mileage": 1245}
>>> k = my_car.get("model")
>>> print(k)
Accord
>>>
```

How to Change Values in a Python Dictionary

To change the value of an item, you once again need to refer to the key name. Here is an example changing the value for the key "year" from 1890 to 2025:

```
$ python3

>>> my_car = {"manufacturer":"Honda", "model": "Accord", "mileage": 1245, "year": 1890}
>>> print(my_car)
{'manufacturer': 'Honda', 'model': 'Accord', 'mileage': 1245, 'year': 1890}
>>> my_car["year"] = 2025
>>> print(my_car)
{'manufacturer': 'Honda', 'model': 'Accord', 'mileage': 1245, 'year': 2025}
>>>
```

How To Loop Through a Python Dictionary

You can use a for loop function to loop through a dictionary in Python. By default, the return value while looping through the dictionary will be the keys of the dictionary. However, there are other methods that can be used to return the values.

Print the Key Names in a Dictionary:

```
$ python3

>>> my_car = {"manufacturer":"Honda", "model": "Accord", "mileage": 1245, "year": 1890}
>>> for k in my_car:
...     print(k)
...
manufacturer
model
mileage
year
>>>
```

By default, the normal for loop will display all the Keys (left side of :) in a Dictionary.

Print the Values in a Dictionary:

```
$ python3

>>> my_car = {"manufacturer":"Honda", "model": "Accord", "mileage": 1245, "year": 1890}
>>> for k in my_car:
...     print(my_car[k])
...
Honda
Accord
1245
1890
>>>
```

Notice how we're using the key to get the value (my_car[k]).

Another way of returning the values by using the **values()** function :

```
$ python3

>>> my_car = {"manufacturer":"Honda", "model": "Accord", "mileage":
1245, "year": 1890}
>>> for k in my_car.values():
...     print(k)
...
Honda
Accord
1245
1890
>>>
```

Print the Keys and Values in a Dictionary:

If you want to Loop through both the keys and the values, you can use the **items()** function

```
$ python3

>>> my_car = {"manufacturer":"Honda", "model": "Accord", "mileage":
1245, "year": 1890}
>>> for k,v in my_car.items():
...     print(k, v)
...
manufacturer Honda
model Accord
mileage 1245
year 1890
>>>
```

Python Programming

Check if a Key Exists in the Dictionary

Here's how you can determine whether a particular key is actually present in the Python dictionary: Say you have to check whether the key "model" is present in the my_car dictionary.

```
$ python3

>>> my_car = {"manufacturer":"Honda", "model": "Accord", "mileage": 1245, "year": 1890}
>>>
>>> if "model" in my_car:
    print("Yes, model is in the dictionary")
  else:
    print("No, model is not in the dictionary")

Yes, model is in the dictionary
>>>
```

How To Determine the Number of Items in the Dictionary

To determine the number of key: value pairs in the dictionary we use one of the most commonly used Python Dictionary methods, **len()**.

```
$ python3

>>> my_car = {"manufacturer":"Honda", "model": "Accord", "mileage": 1245, "year": 1890}
>>>
>>> print(len(my_car))
4
>>>
```

Add an Item to the Python Dictionary

To add a new 'key: value' pair to the dictionary, you have to use a new index key and then assign a value to it.

```
$ python3

>>> my_car = {"manufacturer":"Honda", "model": "Accord", "mileage": 1245, "year": 1890}
>>> print(my_car)
{'manufacturer': 'Honda', 'model': 'Accord', 'mileage': 1245, 'year': 1890}
>>>
>>> my_car["color"] = "blue"
>>>
>>> print(my_car)
{'manufacturer': 'Honda', 'model': 'Accord', 'mileage': 1245, 'year': 1890, 'color': 'blue'}
>>>
```

Removing Items from the Python Dictionary

Here are some of the methods to remove an item from the Python dictionary. Each approaches the same goal from a different perspective.

Method 1 – pop()

The **pop()** method removes the item which has the key name that is being specified. This works well since key names are unique and immutable.

```
$ python3

>>> my_car = {"manufacturer":"Honda", "model": "Accord", "mileage": 1245, "year": 1890}
>>> print(my_car)
{'manufacturer': 'Honda', 'model': 'Accord', 'mileage': 1245, 'year': 1890}
>>>
>>> my_car.pop("model")
'Accord'
>>> print(my_car)
{'manufacturer': 'Honda', 'mileage': 1245, 'year': 1890}
>>>
```

Method 2 – popitem()

> The **popitem()** method removes the item that has been added most recently. In earlier versions, this method used to remove any random item. $ python3
>
> ```
> >>> my_car = {"manufacturer":"Honda", "model": "Accord", "mileage": 1245, "year": 1890}
> >>> print(my_car)
> {'manufacturer': 'Honda', 'model': 'Accord', 'mileage': 1245, 'year': 1890}
> >>>
> >>> my_car.popitem()
> ('year', 1890)
> >>>
> >>> print(my_car)
> {'manufacturer': 'Honda', 'model': 'Accord', 'mileage': 1245}
> >>>
> ```

Method 3 – del()

> Much like the pop() method, the del keyword removes the item whose key name has been mentioned.$ python3
>
> ```
> >>> my_car = {"manufacturer":"Honda", "model": "Accord", "mileage": 1245, "year": 1890}
> >>> print(my_car)
> {'manufacturer': 'Honda', 'model': 'Accord', 'mileage': 1245, 'year': 1890}
> >>>
> >>> del my_car["model"]
> >>> print(my_car)
> {'manufacturer': 'Honda', 'mileage': 1245, 'year': 1890}
> >>>
> ```

Method 4 – del() Entire Dictionary

> Unlike the pop() method, the del keyword can also be used to delete the dictionary altogether. Here's how it can be used to do so: $ python3
>
> ```
> >>> my_car = {"manufacturer":"Honda", "model": "Accord", "mileage": 1245, "year": 1890}
> >>> print(my_car)
> {'manufacturer': 'Honda', 'model': 'Accord', 'mileage': 1245, 'year': 1890}
> >>>
> >>> del my_car
> >>> print(my_car)
> Traceback (most recent call last):
>   File "<stdin>", line 1, in <module>
> NameError: name 'my_car' is not defined
> >>>
> ```

Note that this will cause an error because "my_car" no longer exists.

Method 5 – clear()

The clear() keyword empties the dictionary of all items without deleting the dictionary itself.

> ```
> $ python3
>
> >>> my_car = {"manufacturer":"Honda", "model": "Accord", "mileage": 1245, "year": 1890}
> >>> print(my_car)
> {'manufacturer': 'Honda', 'model': 'Accord', 'mileage': 1245, 'year': 1890}
> >>>
> >>> my_car.clear()
> >>> print(my_car)
> {}
> >>>
> ```

List of Common Python Dictionary Methods

There are a number of Python Dictionary methods that can be used to perform basic operations. Here is a list of the most commonly used ones.

Method	Description
clear()	This removes all the items from the dictionary
copy()	This method returns a copy of the Python dictionary
fromkeys()	This returns a different directory with only the key : value pairs that have been specified
get()	This returns the value of the key mentioned
items()	This method returns the thuple for every key: value pair in the dictionary
keys()	This returns a list of all the Python dictionary keys in the dictionary
popitem()	In the latest version, this method deletes the most recently added item
pop()	This removes only the key that is mentioned
update()	This method updates the dictionary with certain key-value pairs that are mentioned
values()	This method simply returns the values of all the items in the list

Advantages of a Python Dictionary

Here are some of the major pros of a Python library:

a. It improves the readability of your code. Writing out Python dictionary keys along with values adds a layer of documentation to the code. If the code is more streamlined, it is a lot easier to debug. Ultimately, analyses get done a lot quicker and models can be fitted more efficiently.

b. Apart from readability, there's also the question of sheer speed. You can look up a key in a Python dictionary very fast. The speed of a task like looking up keys is measured by looking at how many operations it takes to finish. Looking up a key is done in constant time compared with looking up an item in a large list which is done in linear time.

c. To look up an item in a huge list, the computer will look through every item in the list. If every item is assigned a key-value pair then you only need to look for the key which makes the entire process much faster. A Python dictionary is basically an implementation of a hash table. Therefore, it has all the benefits of the hash table which include membership checks and speedy tasks like looking up keys.

Disadvantages of a Python Dictionary

While a Python dictionary is easily one of the most useful tools, especially for data cleaning and data analysis, it does have a downside. Here are some cons of using a Python dictionary.

a. Dictionaries are unordered. In cases where the order of the data is important, the Python dictionary is not appropriate.

b. Python dictionaries take up a lot more space than other data structures. The amount of space occupied increases drastically when there are many Python Dictionary keys. Of course, this isn't too much of a disadvantage because memory isn't very expensive.

At the end of the day, a Python dictionary represents a data structure that can prove valuable in cleaning data and making it actionable. It becomes even more valuable because it is inherently simple to use and much faster and more efficient as well.

Of course, if you are looking for a career in data science, a comprehensive course with live sessions, assessments, and placement assistance might be just what you need.

Digging Deeper into Python Numbers

Basic Python Numerical Operators

Python is considered a high-level programming language with less complexity when it comes to using the basic operators. It is built to read and implement computer operations easily. Python provides various types of operators for performing numeric tasks and are listed in table form in the Python Operators sections below.

Python Operators

Python Arithmetic Operators

Arithmetic operators help us to do several types of mathematical problems like addition, subtraction, multiplication, exponential values, floor divisions, *etc.*

Let's suppose we have two variables whose values are x = 16, y = 4.

Python Programming

Operator	Description of the operator	Example
Addition (+)	This operator will be adding the values on both sides of operands.	x + y = 20
Subtraction (-)	This operator will be subtracting the right-hand side value from the left-hand side value of the operand.	x – y = 12
Multiplication (*)	This operator will be multiplying the two values on both sides of the operands.	x * y = 64
Division (/)	This operator will be dividing the left-hand side value by the right-hand side value of the operand.	x / y = 4
Modulus (%)	This operator will be dividing the left-hand side value by the right-hand side value of the operand and returns the remainder.	x % y = 0

Exponent (**)	This operator will be doing the 'exponential power' calculation on operands.	x ** y = 16 to the power 4
Floor division (//)	This operator will be dividing the operands, the quotient of a number which is divided by 2 is the result.	13 // 3 = 4, simultaneously 13.0 // 3.0 = 4.0;

Example

Let's see how the output comes. {values in [ ] are outputs}

Let x, y and z be three variables with the following values:

x = 25, y = 30, z = 0:

Python Programming

```
#!/usr/bin/python3

x = 25
y = 30
z = 0

z = x + y
print("result of z is ", z)
z = x - y
print("result of z is ", z)
z = x * y
print("result of z is ", z)
z = x / y
print("result of z is ", z)
z = x % y
print("result of z is ", z)
```

Output:

```
result of z is  55
result of z is  -5
result of z is  750
result of z is  0.8333333333333334
result of z is  25
```

Now suppose

```
#!/usr/bin/python3

a = 4
b = 5
c = a**b

print("value of c is", c)

a = 15
b = 45
c = b//a

print("value of c is", c) )
```

Outputs:

value of c is 1024
 (As 4 to the power 5 is 1024)

value of c is 3
 (As the quotient of 45/15 is 3)

Python Comparison Operators

In Python, comparison operators compare two operands' values and return "True" or "False" depending on whether the condition has matched or not. Another name for Comparison Operators are Python Relational Operator.

Let's take two variables having the values a = 20, b = 15:

Python Programming

Operator	Description of the operator	Example
(==)	This condition becomes true only if two given values (operands) are equal.	(a == b) False
(!=)	This condition becomes true only if the two operands aren't equal.	(a != b) True
(>)	This condition becomes true only if the left operand is greater than the right operand.	(a > b) True
(<)	This condition becomes true only if the right operand is greater than the left operand.	(a < b) False
(>=)	This condition becomes true only if the left operand is greater than or equal to the right operand.	(a >= b) True
(<=)	This condition becomes true only if the right operand is greater than or equal to the left operand.	(a <= b) False

Example

Let's see what the output of the following code is:

```python
#!/usr/bin/python3

i = 10
j = 15

if (i == j):
    print("i is equal to j")
else:
    print("i is not equal to j")
if (i != j):
    print("i is not equal to j")
else:
    print("i is equal to j")
if (i > j):
    print("i is greater than j")
else:
    print("i is not greater than j")
if (i < j):
    print("i is less than j")
else:
    print("i is not less than j")
if (i >= j):
    print("i is greater than or equal to j")
else:
    print("i is neither greater than nor equal to j")
if (i <= j):
    print ("i is less than or equal to j")
else:
    print("i is neither less than nor equal to j")
```

Outputs of the recently used comparison operators:

> *i is not equal to j*
> *i is not equal to j*
> *i is not greater than j*
> *i is less than j*
> *i is neither greater than nor equal to j*
> *i is less than or equal to j*

Python Assignment Operators

These kinds of operators are used to assign several values to the variables. Let's check the different types of assignment operators.

Operator	Description of the operator	Example
Equal (=)	This operator will assign values from right side operand to left side operand.	c = a + b;
Add AND (+=)	This operator will add the right operand with left operand and assigns the sum to the left operand.	c += a [?] it is equivalent to c = c + a;
Subtract AND (-=)	This operator will subtract the right operand from the left operand and assigns the subtraction to the left operand.	c -= a [?] it is equivalent to c = c - a;
Multiply AND (*=)	This operator will multiply the right and left operand and assigns the multiplication to the left operand.	c = a [?] it is equivalent to c = c a;
Divide AND (/=)	This operator will divide the left operand with the right operand and assigns division to the left operand.	c = a [?] it's equivalent to c = ca;

Modulus AND (%=)	This operator takes modulus by using both sides' operand and assigns the outcome to left operand.	c %= a it's equivalent to c = c % a;
Exponent AND (**=)	Does 'to the power' calculation and assigns the outcome to the left operand.	c **= a it's equivalent to c = c**a
Floor division AND (//=)	It does floor division and assigns the outcome to the left operand.	c //= a it's equivalent to c = c // a;

Let's see an example:

```
#!/usr/bin/python3

a = 15
b = 20
c = 0

c = a + b
print("value of c is", c)

c += a
print("value of c is", c)

c *= a
print("value of c is", c)

c %= a
print("value of c is", c)
```

Output: 35, 50, 525, 5 are the outputs of the operators respectively.

Python Bitwise Operators

Bitwise operators are used to perform bit operations. All the decimal values will be converted in the binary format here.

Let us suppose:

> a = 0101 1010
> b = 0001 1000

Then, it will be

> (a & b) = 0001 1000
> (a | b) = 0101 1010
> (a ^ b) = 0100 0010
> (~a) = 1010 0101

Note: There is an in-built function [bin ()] in Python that can obtain the binary representation of an integer number.

Types of Bitwise Operators: [a = 0001 1000, b = 0101 1010]

Operators	Description of the operator	Example
Binary AND (&)	This operator executes a bit if it exists in both operands.	(a & b) is 0001 1000
Binary OR (|)	This operator executes a bit if it exists in one of the operands.	(a | b) is 0101 1010
Binary XOR (^)	This operator executes a bit if it is fixed in one operand but not in both	(a ^ b) is 0100 0010

Binary one's complement (~)	This operator executes just by flipping the bits.	~a = 1110 ~b = 0110
Binary left shift (<<)	This operator executes by moving left operand's value more left. It's specified by the right operand.	a << 100 (means 0110 0000)
Binary right shift (>>)	This operator executes by moving left operand's value right. It's specified by the right operand.	a >> 134 (means 0000 0110)

Let's see an example:

```
#!/usr/bin/python3
a = 50 # 50 = 0011 0010
b = 17 # 17 = 0001 0001
print('a=', a, ':', bin(a), 'b=', b, ':', bin(b))

c = 0
c = a & b; # 16 = 0001 0000
print("result of AND is", c, ':', bin(c))

c = a | b; # 51 = 0011 0011
print("result of OR is", c, ':', bin(c))

c = a ^ b; # 66 = 0100 0010
print("result of XOR is", c, ':', bin(c))
c = a >> 2; # 96 = 0110 0000
print("result of right shift is", c, ':', bin(c))
```

Output:

Result of AND is 16 ? *0b010000*

Result of OR is 51 → 0b110011
Result of XOR is 66 → 0b01000010
Result of right shift is 96 → 0b01100000

Python Logical Operator

The logical operator permits a program to make decisions according to multiple conditions. Every operand is assumed as a condition that can give us a true or false value. There are 3 types of logical operators.

(a = false operand, b = true operand)

Operators	Description of the operator	Example
Logical And(and)	If the given operands both are true, the condition becomes true	Condition is false.
Logical or(or)	If one of the given operands is true, the condition becomes true.	Condition is true.
Logical not(not)	If the given operand is true, the condition becomes false.	Condition is true (for a) and false(for b).

Let's see an example:

```
>>> i = 25
# Logical "and" Example
>>> if i < 30 and i > 18:
    print (" Condition is fulfilled ")
else:
    print(" Condition is not fulfilled ")

# Logical OR Example
>>> if i < 18 or i > 20:
    print(" Condition is fulfilled ")
else:
    print(" Condition is not fulfilled ")
```

Output:

Condition is fulfilled
Condition is fulfilled

Python Membership Operator

Membership operators are operators that validate the membership of a value. It examines for membership in a sequence like strings, lists, tuples, *etc.* Two types of membership operators are:

Operator	Description of Operator	Example
in	The condition becomes true if it can find a variable in a specified sequence.	Follow the example part given below.
not in	The condition becomes true if it can find no variable in a specified sequence.	Follow the example part given below.

Example

```
#!/usr/bin/python3

i = 40
j = 20

listValues = {10, 20, 30, 40}
if (i in listValues):
   print("i is available in the list")
else:
   print("i is not available in the list")
if(j in listValues):
   print("j is available in the list")
else:
   print("j is not available in the list")
k = i / j
if( k in listValues):
   print ("k is available in the list")
else:
   print("k is not available in the list")
```

Output:

i is available in the list
j is available in the list
k is not available in the list

Python Identity Operators

These are operators that are used to determine whether a value is of a particular class or type. To determine the type of data that contains several variables, this type of operator is used. There are two types of Identity operators as shown below:

Operator	Description of the operator	Example
is	The condition becomes true if the variables of each side of the operator are pointing to the same object.	If id(x) and id(y) are equal and x is y, the result is in 1.
Is not	The condition becomes true if the variables of each side of the operator do not point to the same object.	If id(x) and id(y) are not equal and x is not y, the result is not in 1.

Example

```
#!/usr/bin/python3

x = 10
y = 10

print("x = ", x, ':', id(x), "y = ", y, ':', id(y) )
if (x is y):
    print("Both x and y have the same identity")
else:
    print("x and y do not have the same identity")
if( id(x) == id(y) ):
    print("Both x and y have the same identity")
else:
    print("x and y do not have the same identity")
```

Output:

```
x = 10 : 4419156560 y = 10 : 4419156560
Both x and y have the same identity
Both x and y have the same identity
```

Python Operator Precedence

In the below table all the operators from higher to lower precedence are listed

Operator	Description
**	Exponentiation(raise to the power)
~ + -	First one is Complement, second is unary plus and last one is unary minus.
/ * % //	Division, multiplication, modulus, floor division
+ -	Addition and subtraction
>> <<	Right bitwise shift and left bitwise shift
&	Bitwise AND
^ |	Bitwise exclusive OR and bitwise regular OR
<= < > >=	Less than equals to, less than, greater than, greater than equals to (comparison operators)
== <> !=	Equality operators
= %= = /= -= += *= **=	Assignment Operators
is / is not	Identity Operators
in / not in	Membership Operators
not / or / and	Logical Operators

Example

*For example, x = 5 + 14 * 2;*
*In this equation, the value of x is 33, not 38 because the * operator has higher precedence than +.*
*For which it first multiplies 14 * 2 and then adds 5.*

Conditionals

If Statements

In computer programs, code statements are written and often executed sequentially. Sometimes, the execution of code statements might vary depending upon conditions. Let's say this, *If Air Conditioning is not working, call the electrician; otherwise, enjoy the cooling.* When building scripts, we will encounter similar conditions, and that's where the if statement comes into the picture.

Before Jumping to the Conditional Statement, let's quickly scratch the surface of an essential concept of Python that would be handy going forward – indentation.

Python Indentation

We will discuss writing a set/block of Python statements in a few moments. Here, the question is, '**How would the system identify and distinguish the code blocks from one another?**'.

Every programming language has a concept of indentation; it varies depending upon the language but the logic remains the same.

In Python, indentation means adding white space as a prefix to a code statement, and a group of statements with *identical white space* would be considered a single code block as shown below

```
a = 21
b = 11
if a>b:
    print('Var a is greater')
    print('Var b is smaller')
print('Evaluation Completed')
```

In the above example, the first three code statements have the same white space; therefore, these will be referred to as a single code block and executed sequentially and together unless the developer uses some conditional or control structure statement.

However, statements 4 & 5 would be considered a separate code block and executed only when the expression 'a>b' returns **true**.

Finally, the last statement (6) has no extra whitespace; thus, it will be considered part of the first code block.

For the interpreter of the code, the visualisation of the above code would be:

```
Code block 1 {3 statements}
Code block 2 {2 statements}
Code block 1 Continuation {1 statement}
```

If the expression in the 'if' condition returns **true**, the control flow would jump to code block 2 and when finished, then move back to the other statements of code block 1.

Types of Conditional If Statements in Python

The **'if'** statement is used to make a decision between different options and therefore is one of the most useful parts of programming. The Python Operators introduced earlier are commonly used when making decisions.

Python offers a wide range of conditional statements:

- If Statement
- If-else Statement
- if-elif-else Statement

Notice that every other statement is an extended version of the first "**if statement**'. Let's dive deeper into each type in the following sections:

If Statement

The 'if' statement is the most common form of conditional/decision-making statement that developers use to make a decision. Let's understand its syntax:

```
if <expression>:
    [code statements]
```

- **<expression>:** This is the condition that needs to be evaluated, and once done, the system will take the decision. Note that the output of the evaluation will be in a boolean value. Therefore, the result can be either **True** or **False**.

- **[code statements]:** It could contain a set of Python statements; this block will be executed only if the output of the above expression is **True**.

Example:

Python Programming

```
x = 100

if x > 55:
    print("x is greater than 55")
```

In the above code, the value of '**x**' is set to 100. The if condition checks whether the value of '**x**' is greater than 55. In this example, the condition is true and the '**print**' statement of the if block gets executed.

Output:

> x is greater than 55

Consider this example file named show_basic_if_number.py:

```
#!/usr/bin/python3

number1 = 12
number2 = 3
if number1 > number2 :
    print("number1 is greater than number2")
else :
    print("number1 is not greater than number2")
print("Program execution complete")
```

Will result in this when executed

```
$ python3 show_basic_if_number.py
number1 is greater than number2
Program execution complete
$
```

Notice these takeaways from this example

- Even though the "True" code was indented in the program. When the result was printed out as output, it is not indented. To indent the code, we'd need to add white space at the beginning.

- The else condition is not indented. This tells Python that it has the same priority as the "if" statement.

- The else condition code is not executed since the first condition matched (if True)

- "Program execution complete" was printed out because it is not indented and since there are no other conditions to test, the decision is complete. Normal program execution can continue.

So that is the simple if statement. Now let's move to a slightly complex variant of it, i.e., an '**if-else**' statement.

If-else Statement

The above if statement can only execute a single statement or a group of statements based on a single condition. Using the if-else statement, we can handle two conditions.

- • The "else" statement doesn't have a condition. This code executes if no other conditions were true.

You will better understand it once you go through the example listed below. But before that, let's quickly have a look at the syntax:

```
if <expression>:
        [code statements]
else:
        [code statements]
```

In the above syntax, if the '**expression**' placed in the '**if**' statement returns **true**, the code statements of '**if**' block would be executed. In case the '**if**' statement returns **false**, the code statements of the '**else**' block will be executed.

Example:

```
x = 1

if x > 6:
    print("x is greater than 6")
else:
    print("x is less than or equal to 6")
```

In the above example, the value of '**x**' is set to 1; in the '**if**' statement, the condition checks whether '**x**' is greater than 6. Since '**x**' is 1, the condition returns **false** and as a result, the statement of the '**else**' block gets executed.

Output:

x is less than or equal to 6

if-elif-else Statement

So far, we have learned to handle single and two conditions at a time, but often, we are required to work on a group of conditions altogether. In such situations, the 'if-elif-else' statement comes into the picture. The "elif" statement is shorthand for "else if".

Let's quickly have a look at the syntax:

```
if <expression>:
        [code statements]
elif <expression>:
        [code statements]
elif <expression>:
        [code statements]
else:
        [code statements]
```

In '**if-elif-else**' statements, the system will evaluate the '**expression**' sequentially until one of them returns **true**. If the first '**expression**' (if block) returns **true**, all the other '**elif**' statements written below will be skipped, including the '**else**' block. If none of the expressions returns **true**, the '**else**' block will be executed at last.

An example is helpful:

```
x = 101

if x > 105:
    print("x is greater than 105")
elif x > 100:
    print("x is greater than 100 but not greater than 105")
elif x > 5:
    print("x is greater than 5 but not greater than 100")
else:
    print("x is less than or equal to 5")
```

In this example, the value of '**x**' is set to 101.

The first expression of the '**if**' block will check whether the value of '**x**' is greater than 105. If the condition returns **true**, the code statements inside the '**if**' block will be executed.

In case of **false**, the control flow would move to the '**elif**' statement and check its condition.

The control flow will continue checking the conditions until it gets one **true**. As mentioned above, in case none of the conditions returns true, the code statement of the '**else**' block will be executed.

In this example, the second condition returns **true**, and as a result, we will get the following output:

Output:

> *x is greater than 100 but not greater than 105*

Bonus Tip: Other than the three types mentioned above, you can write an **if statement** inside an existing **if statement** if you need to add layers of conditions. This is called a nested if statement and is shown below.

```
if president_first_name == "George" :
    if president_last_name == "Washington":
        print(f"{president_first_name} {president_last_name} was the 1st president of the United States")
    elif president_last_name == "Bush":
        if president_middle_name == "Herbert Walker":
            print(f"{president_first_name} HW {president_last_name} was the 41st president of the United States")
        else:
            print(f"{president_first_name} W {president_last_name} was the 43rd president of the United States")
    elif president_first_name == "Thomas":
    <<and so on>>
```

Functions

When you are working with a language like Python, there will be times when you will need to work with something that is known as a function. These functions are going to be blocks of reusable code that you will use in order to get your specific tasks done, but when you define one of these functions in Python, we need to have a good idea of the two main types of functions that can be used and how each of them works. The two types of functions that are available here are known as built-in and user-defined.

Built-In Functions

The built-in functions are the ones that will come automatically with some of the packages and libraries that are available in Python. An few examples are shown below.

Built-in Functions				
abs()	divmod()	input()	open()	staticmethod()
all()	enumerate()	int()	ord()	str()
any()	eval()	isinstance()	pow()	sum()
basestring()	execfile()	issubclass()	print()	super()
bin()	file()	iter()	property()	tuple()
bool()	filter()	len()	range()	type()
bytearray()	float()	list()	raw_input()	unichr()
callable()	format()	locals()	reduce()	unicode()
chr()	frozenset()	long()	reload()	vars()
classmethod()	getattr()	map()	repr()	xrange()
cmp()	globals()	max()	reversed()	zip()
compile()	hasattr()	memoryview()	round()	__import__()
complex()	hash()	min()	set()	
delattr()	help()	next()	setattr()	
dict()	hex()	object()	slice()	
dir()	id()	oct()	sorted()	

User Defined Functions

We are going to spend our time focusing on user-defined functions because these are the custom ones that the developer will create and use in programs they write. In Python, regardless of what kind of function you are working with, all functions will be treated like objects.

The user-defined functions that we are going to talk about in the next section are going to be important and can really expand out some of the work that we are doing as well. But we also need to take a look at some of the work that we are able to do with our built-in functions as well. The list above includes many of the ones that are found inside of the Python language. Take some time to study them and see what they are able to do to help us get things done.

Why Are User Defined Functions So Important?

- A developer can either write their own functions, known as a user-defined function, or they can use a function from another library (which may not be directly associated with Python). Some characteristics of these user-defined functions include:
    - These functions are reusable code blocks.
    - Once written, you can use them as many times as you need in the code.
    - You can even take that user-defined function and use it in some of your other applications as well.
- These functions is customized by you. You add the functionality you are looking for. You can also modify them anytime if your requirements change.
- Functions are often welcomed by developers because it breaks a large program into smaller pieces. Multiple functions are often easier to maintain than one large piece of code. This means that you are able to support the modular design approach.
- Since a function typically supports a small task, it is much easier to copy

and share with other programs. If you are sharing it with different programs, it may be a good idea to make it into a library so that changes are more easily distributed among different

• A user-defined function that is thoughtfully and well-defined can help ease the process for the development of an application.

Now that we know some advantages of user-defined functions,

Format of a Function

Some of the steps that we need to take in order to write out our own user-defined functions include:

• **Declare your function.** You will need to use the "**def**" keyword to indicate a function is being defined followed immediate by the name of the function.

• **Write out the arguments.** These need to be inside the two parentheses of the function. End this declaration with a **colon** to keep up with the proper Python function declaration.

• **Indent the Statements.** Add the statements that the program is supposed to execute. Similar to if-then statements, the body of the function must be indented from the function declaration.

• **End the function.** You can choose whether you would like to do it with a **return** statement or not. A return indicates what will be returned and if the function call is assigned to a variable, the variable will contain the function return result.

• *def function (argument1, argument2 = "default_arg2"):*
  print(argument1, argument2)

Use of User Defined Function

```
print("Before user defined function")
function("My argument 1", "My argument 2")
print("After user defined function")
# but we can also call the function with a single argument
function("My argument 1 ")
print("After user defined function with only 1 arg")
```

The complete program should look like this and will be named user_defined_function.py:
```
#!/usr/bin/python3

def function (argument1, argument2 = "default_arg2"):
    print(argument1, argument2)


def variable_arg_function (*args):
    print("length of args is ", len(args))
    for i in args:
        print("value is", i)
    return len(args)


print("Before user defined function")
function("My argument 1 ", "My argument_2")
print("After user defined function with 2 args")


# but we can also call the function with a single argument
function("My argument 1 ")
print("After user defined function with only 1 arg")


# calling the function with keywork args
function(argument2="My keyword arg2 ", argument1="My keyword arg1 ")
print("After user defined function with keyword args")


# variable arguments = 4 arguments
arg_len = variable_arg_function("Yes, it is ", True, 10.0, " values")
print("After user defined variable arguments function with ", arg_len, " args")


# variable arguments = 8 arguments
arg_len = variable_arg_function(1, 2, 3, 4, True, False, 8, " values")
print("After user defined variable arguments function with ", arg_len, " args")
```

Output

```
$ python3 user_defined_function.py
Before user defined function
My argument 1  My argument_2
After user defined function with 2 args
My argument 1  default_arg2
After user defined function with only 1 arg
My keyword arg1  My keyword arg2
After user defined function with keyword args
length of args is  4
value is Yes, it is
value is True
value is 10.0
value is  values
After user defined variable arguments function with  4  args
length of args is  8
value is 1
value is 2
value is 3
value is 4
value is True
value is False
value is 8
value is  values
After user defined variable arguments function with  8  args
$
```

Hmm. Let's use this example to examine why we can call this same function with both 2 arguments and with a single argument and how the argument can be in different positions.

Options for Function Arguments

Any time that you are ready to work with these kinds of functions in your code, you will find that they have the ability to work with four types of arguments. These arguments and the meanings behind them are something that will be pre-defined and the developer cannot change them. Instead, the developer is going to have the option to use them but follow the rules that are there with them. You can customize them to make the functions work the way that you want. As we said before, there are four argument types you can work with, and these include:

- **Positional argument:** These values are required and must be passed in the right order and all values must be present when the function is called or the code won't run correctly (you'll get an error when trying to run the program).
    - In the example above, argument1 is required and must be passed in each time.
- **Default argument:** Default arguments indicate a default value for a function argument. If an argument is passed to the function, the passed in value will be used (first example with 2 arguments in example above). If no argument is passed, the function will use the default value for the function. Default values are indicated by the equal sign.
    - In the example above, argument2 is assigned a default value in the function declaration. When only 1 value was passed into the function, the default value was used.
    - Notice the '=' sign is in the function declaration and not in the function call.
    - Default arguments should follow non-default arguments.
- **Keyword arguments:** Sometimes it is helpful to pass the name of the argument in the function caller so it is easier to match with the parameter in the function. The keywords arguments match the name of the parameter in the

function declaration. These keywords will be mapped with the function argument so that you are able to identify all of the values, even if you don't keep the order the same when the code is called.

- The third example shows the use of the keyword argument in the function call. Notice how the arguments are not in the correct order but that is OK because the keyword is used to match the passed in value.

- Notice the '=' sign is in the function call and not in the function declaration. This is how you can tell the difference between a keyword argument and default argument.

- Keyword arguments should follow positional arguments. In other words, any non-keyword arguments need to be in the right position.

- **Variable arguments:** The last argument that we are going to take a look at is the variable number of arguments. This is a good to use when you are not sure how many arguments are going to be necessary for the code that you are writing to pass the function. Passing a '*' **(asterisk)** in front of the parameter indicates a variable argument that you can iterate through. You can use this to design your code where any number of arguments can be passed.

- The fourth and fifth examples show the use of variable arguments in the function call. Notice that in the fourth example 4 values are passed but in the fifth example 8 values are passed *to the same common function*. The function iterates through them printing them all out. The return value is the # of arguments that we can use in the status print out.

Function Return Values

Note that the function return value is can be include (used in the variable parameter function declaration) or not. If it is included, if the function is assigned to a variable, after the function completes, the variable will hold the return value.

- If the return value of the function isn't assigned to a variable, the return data is just discarded.

Print

A **print()** statement is used to deliver information to the user. The print statement typically is composed of objects and uses the "__str__" dunder class method for that object. Think of the parameter that is passed into the **print()** method as being a string. There are different ways of generating this string.

Multiple Object Print

Multiple objects can be passed as parameters to the print() function and they will be parsed into strings and printed out to the terminal. The following example is saved into a file name "print1.py"

```python
#!/usr/bin/python3

user_name = "Bill"
print("The User's name is ", user_name)
```

```
When this is executed, we get the following output$ python3 print1.py
The User's name is  Bill
$
```

The 1st parameter was a string but the 2nd parameter was a variable pointing to a string. The two strings are concatenated together and printed out as a single string.

Printf Style Old String Format - %

An older method of printing variables in a string is known as string interpolation and uses the '%' sign. This is not used as much because better methods such as f-strings below are available but I'm covering it here.

The placeholder actually has the same variable format descriptors as C or C++. The following are just a small sample of the available placeholders but it gives you an idea of what it looks like.

Variable Placeholder	What it describes
d	Signed integer decimal
X	Hexadecimal Upper Case
f	Floating Point decimal
c	Single character
s	String

The following example is saved into a file name "print2.py"

```
#!/usr/bin/python3


user_name = "Bill"
age = 23
print(f"The User's name is %s and his age is %d" % (user_name, age))
```

The values are passed in a tuple because there is more than 1 variable. The "%s" is a placeholder for a string while the "%d" is a placeholder for a decimal value. When this is executed, we get the following output$ python3 print2.py

The User's name is Bill and his age is 23

$

The string is converted and the final string is printed out.

Print String.format

> Another method of printing includes using the string class' **format ()** method. A string can use "{}" as placeholders that are then filled in with values to complete a full string before getting printed out to the terminal. The following example is saved into a file name "print3.py"#!/usr/bin/python3
>
> *user_name = "Bill"*
> *age = 23*
> *print("The User's name is {} and his age is {} ".format(user_name, age))*

> When this is executed, we get the following output$ python3 print3.py
> *The User's name is Bill and his age is 23*
> *$*

The 1st placeholder of the string holds the user_name (1st parameter passed to format() function). The 2nd placeholder of the string holds the age (2nd parameter passed to format() function)

Print f-strings

> A new and **preferred method of printing strings uses f-strings**. An f-string is preceded by a f before the opening parenthesis (f"). The placeholders in the string actually hold the variable names making the string easy to read and interpret. The following example is saved into a file name "print4.py"#!/usr/bin/python3
>
> *user_name = "Bill"*
> *age = 23*
> *print(f"The User's name is {user_name} and his age is {age}")*

> Note the string is preceded by an f. When this is executed, we get the following output$ python3 print4.py
> *The User's name is Bill and his age is 23*
> *$*

The "**{user_name}**" placeholder of the string is created from the user_name variable. The "**{age}**" placeholder of the string is created from the age variable.

Input and Output

So far, we've only been writing programs that only use data we have explicitly defined in the script. However, your programs can also take in input from the user and utilize it. Python lets us solicit inputs from the user with a very intuitively named function—the input () function. Writing out the code input () enables us to prompt the user for information, which we can further manipulate. We can take the user input and save it as a variable, print it straight to the terminal, or do anything else we might like.

When we use the input function, we can pass in a string. The user will see this string as a prompt, and their response to the prompt will be saved as the input value. For instance, if we wanted to query the user for their favorite food, we could write the following:

```
>>> favorite_food = input("What is your favorite food? ")
What is your favorite food? Thai
>>> print(favorite_food)
Thai
>>>
```

If you ran this code example, you would be prompted for your favorite food. You could save multiple variables this way and print them all at once using the **print ()** function along with print formatting, as we covered earlier. To be clear, the text that you write in the input function is what the user will see as a prompt; it isn't what you are inputting into the system as a value.

Notice the space after the '?' but before the ending " in the prompt above. If you didn't include that, the answer that you type will be squished beside the '?'.

When you run the code above, you'll be prompted for an input. After you type in some text and hit the return key, the text you wrote will be stored as the variable **favorite_food**.

The input command can only have 1 parameter so this is not allowed because there are 3 parameters being passed - the first string, the user_name, and the 2nd string.

```
>>> user_name = "Bob"
>>> favorite_food = input("What is ", user_name, "'s favorite food? ")
What is Bob's favorite food? Italian
>>> print(favorite_food)
Italian
>>>
```

The input command can be used along with string formatting to inject variable values into the text that the user will see. For instance, if we had a variable called **user_name** that stored the name of the user, we could structure the input statement using an f-string like this:

```
>>> user_name = "Bob"
>>> favorite_food = input(f"What is {user_name}'s favorite food? ")
What is Bob's favorite food? Italian
>>> print(favorite_food)
Italian
>>>
```

Printing and Formatting Outputs

We've already dealt with the **print ()** function quite a bit, but let's take some time to address it again here and learn a bit more about some of the more advanced things you can do with it.

By now, you've gathered that it prints whatever is in the parentheses to the terminal. Besides, you've learned that you can format the printing of statements with either the modulus operator (%), the format function (. format ()) or preferably the f-string.

Long Strings

However, what should we do if we need to print a very long message?

In order to prevent a long string from running across the screen, we can use triple quotes that surround our string. Printing with triple quotes allows us to separate our print statements onto multiple lines. For example, we could print like this:

> *>>> print('''By using triple quotes, we can*
> *... divide our print statement into multiple*
> *... lines, making it easier to read. ''')*
> *By using triple quotes, we can*
> *divide our print statement into multiple*
> *lines, making it easier to read.*
> *>>>*

Escape Characters

What if we need to print characters that are equivalent to string formatting instructions? For example, if we ever needed to print out the characters "%s "or "%d , " we would run into trouble. If you recall, these are string formatting commands, and if we try to print these out, the interpreter will interpret them as formatting commands.

Here's a practical example. As mentioned, typing "/t" in our string will put a tab in the middle of our string. Assume we type the following:

> \>\>\> *print("We want a \t here, not a tab.")*
> *We want a   here, not a tab.*
> \>\>\>

Notice the big gap between a and here - it is inserting a tab which isn't what we want.

By using an escape character, we can tell Python to include the characters that come next as part of the string's value. The escape character we want to use is the "raw string" character, an "r" before the first quote in a string, like this:

> \>\>\> *print(r"We want a \t here, not a tab.")*
> *We want a \t here, not a tab.*
> \>\>\>

The "raw string" formatter enables you to put any combination of characters you'd like within the string and have it to be considered part of the string's value.

However, what if we did want the tab in the middle of our string? In that case, using special formatting characters in our string is referred to as using **"escape characters."** "Escaping" a string is a method of reducing the ambiguity in how characters are interpreted. When we use an escape character, we escape the typical method that Python uses to interpret certain characters, and the characters we type are understood to be part of the string's value. The escape primarily used in Python is the backslash (\). The backslash prompts Python to listen for a unique character to follow that will translate to a specific string formatting command.

We already saw that using the "\t" escape character puts a tab in the middle of our string, but there are other escape characters we can use as well.

Escape Character	What it Does

Python Programming

\n	Starts a new line (Line Feed)
\t	Prints a tab (Spaces)
\\	Prints a backslash itself
\"	Prints out a double quote instead of a double quote marking the end of a string
\'	Prints out a single quote instead of a single quote marking the end of a character or string.

Input and Formatting Exercise

Let's do another exercise that applies what we've covered in this section. You should try to write a program that does the following:

- Prompts the user for answers to several different questions.
- Prints out the answers on different lines using a single print statement.

Give this a shot before you look below for an answer to this exercise prompt.

If you've given this a shot, your answer might look something like this:

```
#!/usr/bin/python3

favorite_food = input ("What's your favorite food? ")
favorite_animal = input ("What about your favorite animal? ")
favorite_movie = input ("What's the best movie? ")
print (f"Favorite food is: {favorite_food}\n" +
    f"Favorite animal is: {favorite_animal}\n" +
    f"Favorite movie is: {favorite_movie}")
```

And the output would look like:

```
$ python3 input1.py
What's your favorite food? Thai
What about your favorite animal? zebra
What's the best movie? Yes Man
Favorite food is: Thai
Favorite animal is: zebra
Favorite movie is: Yes Man
$
```

Loops in Python

Loops in any programming language enable you to execute a particular code block multiple times based on your desired condition/expression. Loops help you iterate through every element of an object, array, list, tuple and even string.

From a developer's perspective, loops are an essential programming concept; every developer must master them.

Let's dive into the details of loops.

Why are loops used?

As mentioned above, loops help you automate repetitive tasks. It makes your code easy to read and efficient. Along with these, loops allow you to cycle through every item inside objects like arrays, lists, dictionaries, and tuples.

Now, Since we know the purpose of loops, let's explore different types of loops offered by Python.

Types of Loops in Python

Python primarily offers the following types of loops:

- *for* loop
- *while* loop

We will learn about both, along with some examples.

For Loops

The "for" loop in Python is used to iterate through iterable objects. For instance, to traverse through every string character, you can use a for loop in Python. Yes! A *string* is one of the iterable objects in Python. A few more are listed below:

- Lists
- Tuples
- Dictionary
- Sets

Using a for loop, you can iterate sequentially through elements of the above-listed iterable objects. Let's have a look at the syntax of for loop.

For Loop Syntax

> *for arbitrary_variable in iterable_object:*
>   *Code statement*

- **arbitrary _variable**: It represents a variable that would sequentially iterate through the object stored in iterable_object, and in each iteration, it points towards a particular item of the object.

- **iterabe_object**: As mentioned above, it could be a list, tuple, string, dictionary, set or any iterable object.
- The **code statement** is the loop's body that gets executed in each iteration.

Let's quickly have a look at a few examples of for loops:

Example #1: for Loop with a String

```
# Iterating through a string using a for loop
string = "Hello, World!"
for eachitem in string:
    print(eachitem)
```

In this example, we have a string variable named *string* with the value "Hello, World!". The for loop iterates over each character in the string and prints it on a separate line. The *for* loop variable, *eachitem* stores the characters of the string in every iteration and prints the same.

Output:

```
H
e
l
l
o
,

W
o
r
l
d
!
```

Example #2: for Loop with a List

In this example, we have a list object named *fruits* that contains a few names of fruits as values. The *for* loop iterates over each element in the list and prints it on a separate line.

```
# Iterating through a list using a for loop
fruits = ["apple", "banana", "orange", "grape"]
for fruit in fruits:
    print(fruit)
```

During each iteration, the loop variable *fruit* holds each item from the list.

Output:

> *apple*
> *banana*
> *orange*
> *grape*

Example #3: for Loop with a tuple

Tuples and Lists are similar to each other. In the above example, we have a tuple named *numbers* that contain a sequence of numbers (1-5). The *for* loop iterates over each element in the tuple and prints it on a separate line.

```
# Iterating through a tuple using a for loop
numbers = (1, 2, 3, 4, 5)
for num in numbers:
    print(num)
```

The loop variable *num* holds each item from the tuple on each iteration.

Output:

Python Programming

```
1
2
3
4
5
```

Example #4: for Loop with a dictionary

In this example, we have a dictionary named *student_sub_grades* that contains students' grades as **value** and their names as **keys**.

The **for** loop iterates over each **key-value** pair in the dictionary. To do so, we have used the *items()* method, and the loop variables *student* and *grade* capture the key and value of each item, respectively.

```
# Iterating over a dictionary using a for loop
student_sub_grades = {"John": 85, "Emma": 92, "Michael": 78, "Sophia": 95}
for student, grade in student_sub_grades.items():
    print(student, ":", grade)
```

The loop body has a print statement displaying the student's name and grades.

Output:

> *John : 85*
> *Emma : 92*
> *Michael : 78*
> *Sophia : 95*

for Loop with range() method

Other than elements of the above-mentioned iterable objects, the *for* loops can also be used to iterate through a sequence of numbers. To generate a sequence, *the range()* method is used.

Before jumping to the example, let's quickly learn about the *range()* method.

Range Syntax:

> *range(start, stop, step)*

- **start** represents the starting number in the sequence. It's an optional parameter. In case none is passed, 0 would be considered as default.
- **stop** represents the last number in the sequence. It's a required parameter.
- **step** represents the difference/step between two adjacent numbers in the sequence. It's an optional parameter, and the default value is 1.

A for loop with the *range()* method allows you to repeat the execution of the

loop body a certain number of times.

Now, let's see the *for* loop with range() in action:

> In this example, the *range(1, 6)* method generates numbers from 1 to 5 (inclusive).
>
> *# Iterating through a range of numbers using a for loop*
>
> *for num in range(1, 6):*
>
>   *print(num)*

The *for* loop iterates over each number in the sequence and *prints* it on a separate line.

Output

> *1*
> *2*
> *3*
> *4*
> *5*

Commonly used Keywords in the for Loop

In the loop body, often, you will see that a set of keywords are used to enhance the functionality of the loop or to skip a few code statements during execution.

In this section, we will learn about three commonly used keywords that would be handy to you while handling complex conditions in the loop body.

The continue Keyword

The **continue** keyword is used in a loop body to skip the execution of code written after the keyword in the current iteration, and the control flow will move to the next iteration directly.

When the **continue** keyword is encountered, the loop will immediately move to the next iteration, skipping the remaining code statements of the current iteration.

We use the **continue** keyword mainly when we want to skip the execution of a few code statements based on some condition.

The break Keyword

The **break** keyword is used in a loop to exit the loop. When a **break** statement is encountered, the control flow will immediately skip the further iterations of the loop and move to the next code statement written **outside** the loop body.

As mentioned above, we use the break keyword to **exit** the loop when a condition is met.

The pass keyword

The **pass** keyword is used as a placeholder when code statements are syntactically required in the loop body, but you don't want any code or action to be executed. It works like a null statement.

It is often used as a temporary placeholder for a particular code you intend to write later.

Let's see these three keywords in action:

Example #5: for loop with continue, break and pass Keyword

```
numbers = [1, 2, 3, 4, 5]

# Example using continue
print("Example using continue:")
for num in numbers:
    if num == 2:
        continue  # Skip the iteration when num is 2
    if num == 3:
        pass #does nothing when num is 3
    if num == 4:
        break #Exist the loop when num is 4
    print(num)
```

In the above example, the **continue** keyword will **skip the loop iteration**. So when **num** is 2, the loop skips the remaining code statements and moves to the next iteration, i.e., 2 won't be printed in the output.

The **pass** keyword is used as a placeholder when the *num* is 3. It won't affect the order of execution, but later in future, you can replace the pass keyword with the required code statements.

The **break** keyword will **exit the loop** when the num is 4. Therefore the last iteration, i.e., num = 5, will never occur.

Output of the above code:

```
1
3
```

While Loops

So far, we have learned about the *for* loop and saw that *for* loop works well in situations where we know the number of iterations/ times the code needs to be executed.

In contrast, we use the **while** loop **when the number of iterations is not defined**. The loop's code block will be executed until the specified **condition** is true.

Let's understand the syntax of the **while** loop:

While Loop Syntax

```
while condition:
    Code statements
```

Here,

- **condition** is a desired expression that is evaluated before every iteration, and if the result of the evaluation is **False**, the code statements written in the loop won't be executed. Control **flow** will exist in the loop. In case of **True** output, the code block will be executed.

- The execution of the code block will take place until a single False is encountered in the condition.

Let's have a look at the example:

Example #7: while Loop with a simple condition

```
count = 0
while count < 7:
    print("Count:", count)
    count += 1
```

In this example, the while loop is executed as long as the value of the variable count is less than 7. Initially, the count is 0.

The loop executes the body 7 times because the count increments by 1 with each iteration.

Once the count becomes 7, the condition count < 7 becomes false, and the loop is exited.

Output:

```
Count: 0
Count: 1
Count: 2
Count: 3
Count: 4
Count: 5
Count: 6
```

Note: While writing a *while* loop, you must ensure that the condition eventually returns a *False* to **prevent infinite iterations**.

Python Modules

Modules consist of Python code (program body, functions, variables) that are bundled together. Modules can be shared between different programs. As your Python program gets larger, it would be useful to split the large file into smaller files. But how are these smaller files combined? That is where modules come in.

Python Program Structure

Below is a picture that shows 2 custom modules and one standard library module.

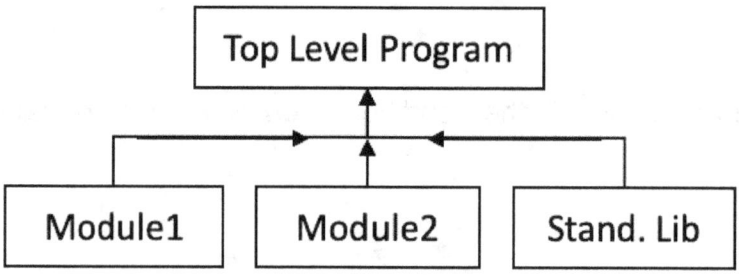

You can see how the different modules and the Standard Library module feed into the Top Level Program.

Python Shared Functions

Assume you had a written a program named **amazon_ebay.py** that contained 10

Python functions that connect and gather information from Amazon or eBay. If you also had 5 different programs that connect to Amazon or eBay, you have 2 choices:

1. Duplicate the 10 functions in **amazon_ebay.py** in each of your 5 programs.

2. Find a way for each of the 5 programs to share the functions in **amazon_ebay.py**.

Now both methods are possible but what if Amazon changes the functionality of 2 of the programs?

- In case 1, you would need to change the code in all 5 programs for a total of 10 changes (5 x 2).

- In case 2, you only need to make 2 changes - in the amazon_ebay.py file.

Most people would choose option 2 to reduce the number of changes and therefore work.

Module Import

The keyword **import** is used to import the functions and definitions from a Python file/module. You may have already been importing the Python Standard Library functions without knowing it. For instance, the **sys** Standard Library is sometimes used to exit a function and return an error code.

```
import sys

if discovered_big_error:
    sys.exit(-1)
else
    sys.exit(0)
```

It is standard practice to leave a blank line between the imports at the top and the first line of code.

In this example, we import the **sys** module and then we test to see if a big error was discovered. If discovered_big_error is True, we call the **exit()** function that is part of the **sys** module which will exit and issue a return code of -1.

Notice the syntax that calls the **exit** function of the **sys** module. There is a dot separating the module name and the function name - **sys.exit(return parameter)**

Finding the Module File

How is the module file discovered? With any Python code import, the process is as follows:

> 1) The Python interpreter searches the file system starting in the current directory where it is executed (Top Level Program)

> 2) Then, the interpreter searches for its predefined paths in its configuration. One example of a predefined path is the **PYTHONPATH** environment variable.

If the module to be imported is in the same directory as the Top Level Program file, the import is straightforward. Just import the name of the file (leaving off the .py suffix).

Case #1 requires a little more explanation but this is the most common way of creating modules because it is helpful to segment modules based on function. For instance, if you have a **car.py** Top Level Program, I'd like to have a subdirectory named **drivetrain** and a subdirectory named **body**. Calling the **tree** command shows us the tree view of the directory. Notice the **car.py** is in the main directory and parts associated with each section of the vehicle are in the appropriate directory.

What Happens When a Matched Module File is Found?

- When a match is found (the name of the module), the interpreter automatically executes it from start to finish.

- When importing a module for the first time, Python will generate a compiled .pyc extension file. This file is then used on subsequent calls because it executes faster.

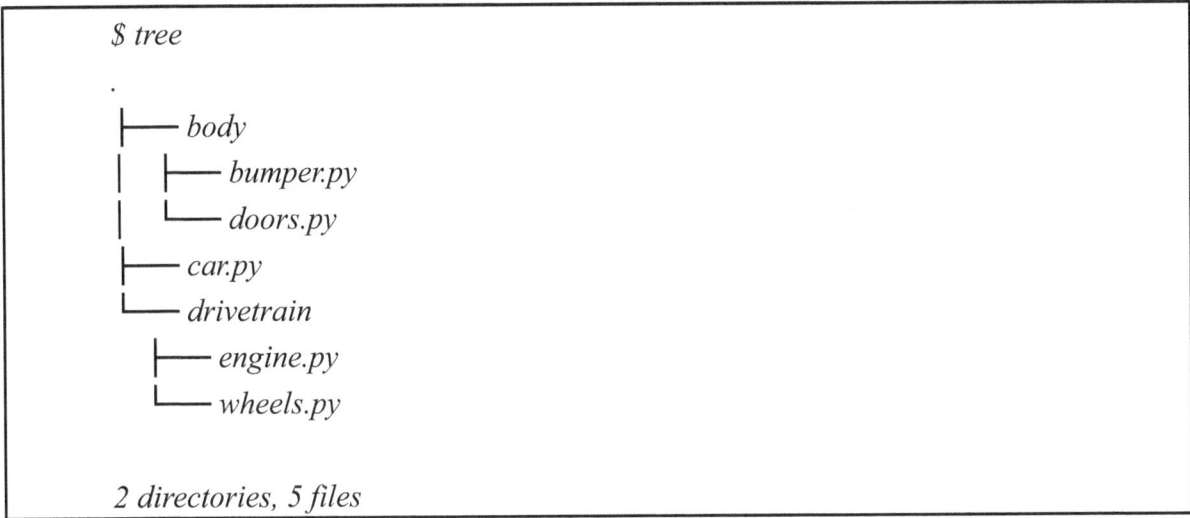

An example of the imports at the top of the car.py file are shown below along with a few functions from the modules. Notice how the path to the file is separated by '.' where the '/' would normally be.

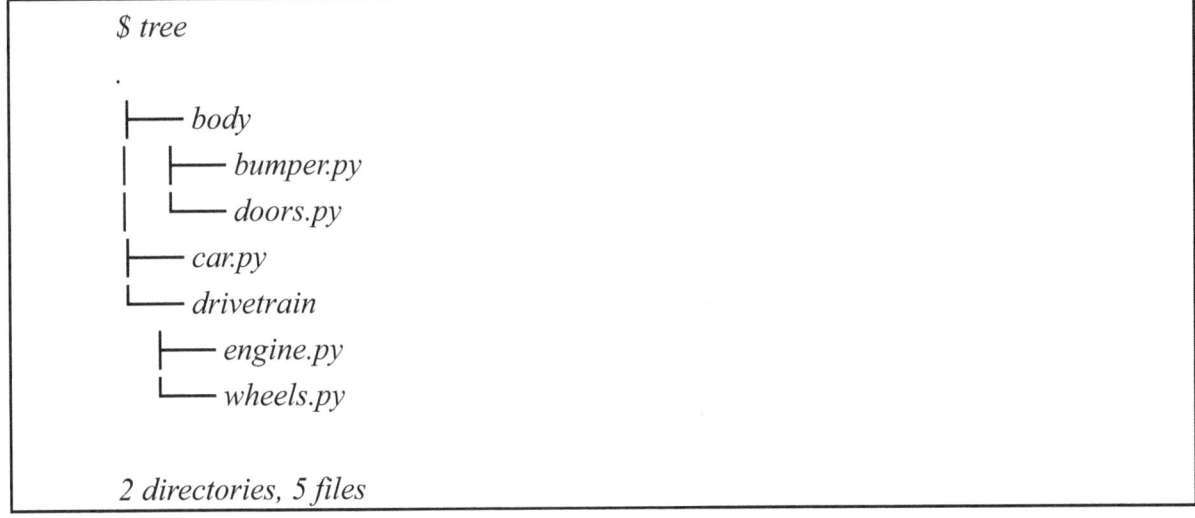

Let's look at the content of these files:

car.py

```
#!/usr/bin/python3
import body.doors
import drivetrain.engine
import drivetrain.wheels

car_type = "sedan"
car_power = "cruising"
car_doors = "2 door"

car = "2016 Mustang"
if drivetrain.wheels.size(car) > 20.5:
    car_type = "monster truck"

if drivetrain.engine.size(car) > 4.5:
    car_power = "racing"

if body.doors.num_doors(car) == "4":
    car_doors = "4 door"

print(f"Car model {car} is {car_type} with {car_doors} and is good for {car_power}")
```

Things to notice:

- The function call has '.' separators just like the import. Python needs that path to find the correct function.

- There are 2 functions with the same name - **size()**. However, the path to them is different so this isn't a problem - they are distinct functions.

Looking closer at the imported files...

drivetrain/wheels.py

```python
#!/usr/bin/python3

def size(car):
    if car == "2016 Mustang":
        return 16.25
    elif car == "2018 Dodge Ram":
        return 20.15
    elif car == "1996 Geo Prism":
        return 14.65
```

drivetrain/engine.py

```python
#!/usr/bin/python3

def size(car):
    if car == "2016 Mustang":
        return 5.0
    elif car == "2018 Dodge Ram":
        return 5.5
    elif car == "1996 Geo Prism":
        return 1.6
```

body/doors.py

```python
#!/usr/bin/python3

def num_doors(car):
    if car == "2016 Mustang":
        return 2
    elif car == "2018 Dodge Ram":
        return 2
    elif car == "1996 Geo Prism":
        return 4
```

And then running the program, we get this output

```
$ python3 car.py
Car model 2016 Mustang is sedan with 2 door and is good for racing
$
```

Python Package

Files in Python hold modules and directories are stored in packages. A single package in Python holds similar modules (or files). Therefore, a single Python package could contain modules that are similar. For instance the **drivetrain** directory has a **engine.py** file and a **wheels.py** file.

Every Python package needs to have a *__init__.py* file in the directory. Typically, these can be empty files but they indicate the directory could be a package. So if we wanted to create a package named **drivetrain** we need to add an empty *__init__.py* file. The imports that are being used are also compiled into .pyc files making the **tree** command return:

```
.
├── body
│   ├── __init__.py
│   ├── __pycache__
│   │   └── doors.cpython-39.pyc
│   ├── bumper.py
│   └── doors.py
├── car.py
└── drivetrain
    ├── __init__.py
    ├── __pycache__
    │   ├── engine.cpython-39.pyc
    │   └── wheels.cpython-39.pyc
    ├── engine.py
    └── wheels.py

4 directories, 10 files
```

Now that we have created a package, we can make use of another style to make the

Python Programming

import a little simpler. We can specify just the file we want from the package using a **from <package> import <filename>** style. This means the function calls in the **if** statements need to change as well (remove the starting "body." and the "drivetrain.")

car.py

```
#!/usr/bin/python3
from body import doors
from drivetrain import engine, wheels

car_type = "sedan"
car_power = "cruising"
car_doors = "2 door"

car = "2016 Mustang"
if wheels.size(car) > 20.5:
    car_type = "monster truck"

if engine.size(car) > 4.5:
    car_power = "racing"

if doors.num_doors(car) == "4":
    car_doors = "4 door"

print(f"Car model {car} is {car_type} with {car_doors} and is good for {car_power}")
```

Objects, Methods, and Inheritance

Object-oriented programming (OOP) is a programming paradigm in which programs are modeled according to their properties and behaviors rather than functions and logic.

All these elements are then bundled into objects.

Let's say, for example, an object could be you or me in real life.

It could be a person with a valid name, age, birth date, occupation, and other data or **properties** in terms of programming languages.

Also, we have certain **behaviors**. We can walk, talk, work, sleep, jog, and others as well.

So, OOP allows us to program and model real-world elements and make them as realistic and meaningful as possible.

Each entity in the world can be modeled as a Python object which possesses some data and does some function (has some behavior).

What have we been doing till now?

It's the procedural programming paradigm.

It provides steps, functions, and code blocks that follow a sequential order of completing commands.

Let's take a look at the most basic concepts of OOP; *Classes*.

Classes and Objects

To model real-world objects in programming, we need a blueprint of these objects or a prototype on which these objects will be based on.

Classes are basically user-defined blueprints that state how an object should look, what attributes or properties its object should have, and what it should do (the behaviors).

Basically, we describe the general behavior each object of a class can have.

What are objects?

Objects are *instances* of a class, that we work with, in life and programs.

This process, making objects from classes, is called instantiation.

Let's take an example under consideration.

If you've ever come across a car, let's see what attributes it can have.

The color, number of tires, a model of the car, engine specifications, and others.

When we program our class called *Car*, these will act as the properties of our car.

Now, what does the car do?

It drives, honks, and performs other functions internally.

*These are the **properties** or methods of our **class** Car.*

See, how every car performs these actions and has these properties; ***Classes are general representations of real-world objects.***

Objects are the specific instances of these classes and have relevant data in them.

For example, a Ford Mustang will be different from an SUV and have massively different properties.

Both of them are individual objects from our class Car.

Writing Classes

Let's head back to our editor and code an example class with properties and behaviors.

Here's the code: (don't stress, I'll explain everything later)

```python
class Car:
    '''Modelling a car'''

    def __init__(self, model, license):
        '''Initialize all attributes and properties'''
        self.model = model
        self.license = license

    def drive(self):
        print("Vroom vroom! The car drives!")

    def honk(self):
        print("HONK! HONK!")


# Create the cars now
# Create a Ford Mustang
ford_mustang = Car("ford-8", "AX-2939")
# Create a Honda SUV
honda_suv = Car("Honda", "MX-2101")
```

Now, on to the analysis of the code we just wrote.

An Explanation on Classes (Code Breakdown)

We begin by defining our class on line one using the *class* keyword and immediately following it is the name of the class.

Conventionally, we start the name of the class in uppercase letters.

In line 2, we define a ***docstring***.

It is a simple statement that tells us more about what the class has to offer or what it does.

On line 4, we finally define a function, since we know that functions are defined using the **def** keyword.

All functions defined in a class are called ***methods*** of that class.

The __*init*__ is a special method provided by Python for every class, which, upon the instantiation process, runs automatically (when you create a new object).

A question you might have: Why the underscores?

They are to help you understand that it is a default function provided by Python and it shouldn't conflict with your own special function names.

Now, it takes in three parameters in our case, but it can have as many parameters as you want.

The ***self*** parameter is necessary and should come before others.

What is self?

The **self** keyword is a reference that helps objects refer to themselves anywhere in the class.

It allows objects to have individual access to all the properties and methods defined in the class and doesn't interfere with other objects.

The self keyword is automatically passed whenever an object is made, and all other parameters can be passed with it (optional, but if used in the class declaration, they must be provided).

Now, on line 6 & 7, we prefix each parameter with **self**.

This is so each object of the class has its own attributes (specific to it) and can be used throughout the class for that object only.

Next, we define two other functions (lines 9 and 12) and pass the **self** parameter to it, which is necessary, so each object has access to its own methods.

This is it for our class; let's see what happens next.

Making an Instance: Objects

Outside of the scope of the class, we are finally using our class to make objects of it (or cars out of the class Car).

These are basically instructions for how our class should behave for a specific car.

We can make an object using this syntax:

> *objectOfTheClass = nameOfClass('param1', 'param2', ...)*

Let's see how we did it for our example:

> *# Create a Ford Mustang*
> *ford_mustang = Car("ford-8", "AX-2939")*
>
> *# Create a Honda SUV*
> *honda_suv = Car("Honda", "MX-2101")*

We ask Python to make a car whose model is something and the license is something else. This of this like a cookie cutter. The cookie may look the same (variations of a car) but the decorations and frosting of the cookie can change.

Again, we ask Python to make a different car with different data.

How does it work?

As soon as you instantiate an object and assign it, the interpreter runs the __int__ function and assigns **self** to the newly made object and also associates the passed arguments to the parameters.

The __init__ method then returns an object and it is assigned to our variable ford_mustang.

Now, let's use this object to see what attributes or properties our objects have.

Accessing Attributes and Methods

Try running the following code after instantiating your class:

```
print(ford_mustang.model)

print(ford_mustang.license)
```

It prints what we sent to it using the arguments in our class.

As they are associated with our object now, the self.model is used to send back the data to us.

Here's the output:

> *ford-8*
> *AX-2939*

If you ask for these attributes from the second object, the output will be what you sent with it.

> *print(honda_suv.model)*
>
> *print(honda_suv.license)*

It prints what we sent to it using the arguments in our class.

As they are associated with our object now, the self.model is used to send back the data to us.

Here's the output:

> *Honda*
> *MX-2101*

Now, if you want to access the methods, simply use the dot operator again use the methods.

Here's how:

> *print(ford_mustang.honk())*

Outputs

```
HONK! HONK!
None
```

'**None**' is actually the return statement which is executing and printing as well.

Let's write a new method and use an attribute to see different outputs for different objects: (Add to your car class from the last example)

```python
def mileage(self):
    val = input("What is the mileage? ")
    print(self.model + " Mileage: " + val)
```

Which will make the Car class look like this;

```python
class Car:
    '''Modelling a car'''

    def __init__(self, model, license):
        '''Initialize all attributes and properties '''
        self.model = model
        self.license = license

    def drive(self):
        print("Vroom vroom! The car drives!")

    def honk(self):
        print("HONK! HONK!")

    def mileage(self):
        val = input("What is the mileage? ")
        print(self.model + " Mileage: " + val)

# Create the cars now
# Create a Ford Mustang
ford_mustang = Car("ford-8", "AX-2939")
# Create a Honda SUV
honda_suv = Car("Honda", "MX-2101")
```

When you run this on a class, you will be prompted to enter a value since we use the *input() function.*

Enter the value and let's check the output:

```python
print(ford_mustang.mileage())
```

Output

> *What is the mileage? 2200*
> *ford-8 Mileage: 2200*
> *None*

Let's take a look at some other concepts for Object-oriented programming, next.

This chapter covers a little more advanced topics from object-oriented programming like inheritance, child classes, and others.

Also, we'll see how to import classes just like we imported modules.

Inheritance

In real-world situations, most objects have a relationship to other objects.

Similarly, if we want a specialized version of a more general element, this programming concept is called *Inheritance,* where a child class grabs all properties and methods from the parent class and makes use of them and adds something of its own.

The parent class is the class which is more general and has all the basic functions.

For example, if we wrote the code for a Car, it is pretty general.

If now, we wish to write a class for an *electric car*, it will inherit most of the properties and behaviors from the parent (Car) class and add more stuff of its own.

Let's take a look at child classes next.

Child Classes: Writing One

We'll model an electric car, a more specific form of our Car class.

Here's the code and let's analyze it afterwards:

```python
class Car:
    '''Modelling a car'''

    def __init__(self, model, license):
        '''Initialize all attributes and properties'''
        self.model = model
        self.license = license

    def drive(self):
        print("Vroom vroom! The car drives!")

    def honk(self):
        print("HONK! HONK!")

    def mileage(self):
        val = input("What is the mileage? ")
        print(self.model + " Mileage: " + val)

class ElectricCar(Car):
    def __init__(self, model, license):
        super().__init__(model, license)

# Create a Tesla X electric car now
tesla_x = ElectricCar("Tesla", "AA-9323")

print(tesla_x.mileage())
print(tesla_x.model)
```

Output

> *What is the mileage? 343*
> *Tesla Mileage: 343*
> *None*
> *Tesla*

Firstly, we write our child class and use the parenthesis to set the tesla_x variable to ElectricCar().

Next, we declare the __*init*__ function for ElectricCar() just like we did for the Car() class and pass to it the parameters and the self keyword that refer to the object.

Next, something different.

We use the **super()** function and use the ElectricCar's __**init**__ method to refer to the __*init*__ *method of the parent class.*

This is done so a connection can be made between the parent class and the child class, and after this **super()** call, it can access all attributes and methods of the parent class.

Although ElectricCar doesn't have any methods of its own right now, one could definitely be added in later. A method that is specific for electric cars would be appropriate here.

Next, we make an object of our new ElectricCar class and call the methods and attributes which created expected output since now, a relationship is made between the *parent and child or super and subclass.*

If you decide to assign methods to the child class, remember, the parent class can't access them.

But, the child class can definitely (always) access the methods of the parent class.

Importing Classes

As your programs grow, so will the complexity, both in logic and file size.

It is always recommended to ship your classes as individual files and import them wherever they are required.

This is possible using the **import** statements we studied in the modules section.

Assuming the class is stored in a filename car.py , here's how you can import the classes into another file and use them properly:

```
from car import Car
from car import ElectricCar
# Import both on the same line.
from car import Car, ElectricCar
from car import *
import car
```

Review

We've covered a lot of ground in the first section of this book. We'll begin covering some more complex topics and concepts. However, before we move on, let's be sure that we've got the basics down. You won't learn the new concepts unless you are familiar with what we've covered so far, so for that reason, let's do a quick review of what we've learned so far:

- **Variables**: Variables are representations of values. They contain the value and allow the value to be manipulated without having to write it out every time. Variables must contain only letters, numbers, or underscores. Besides, the first character in a variable cannot be a number, and the variable name must not be one of Python's reserved keywords.

- **Operators**: Operators are symbols, which are used to manipulate data. The assignment operator (=) is used to store values in variables. Other operators in Python include: the addition operator (+), the subtraction operator (-), the multiplication operator (*), the division operator (/), the floor division operator (//), the modulus operator (%), and the exponent operator (**). The mathematical operators can be combined with the assignment operator. (Ex. +=, -=, *=).

- **Strings**: Strings are text data, declared by wrapping text in single or double-quotes. There are two methods of formatting strings; with the modulus operator or the. format () command. The "s," "d," and "f" modifiers are used to specify the placement of strings, integers, and floats.

- **Integers**: Integers are whole numbers, numbers that possess no decimal points or fractions. Integers can be stored in variables simply by using the assignment operator.

- **Floats**: Floats are numbers that possess decimal parts. The method of creating a float in Python is the same as declaring an integer, just choose a name for the variable and then use the assignment operator.

- **Type Casting**: Type casting allows you to convert one data type to another if the conversion is feasible (non-numerical strings cannot be converted into integers or floats). You can use the following functions to convert data types: int (), float (), and str ().

- **Lists**: Lists are just collections of data, and they can be declared with brackets and commas separating the values within the brackets. Empty lists can also be created. List items can be accessed by specifying the position of the desired item. The append () function is used to add an item to a list, while the del command and remove () function can be used to remove items from a list.

- **List Slicing**: List slicing is a method of selecting values from a list. The item at the first index is included, but the item at the second index isn't. A third value, a stepper value, can also be used to slice the list, skipping through the array at a rate specified by the value. (Ex. - numbers [0:9:2])

- **Tuples**: Tuples are like lists, but they are immutable; unlike lists, their contents cannot be modified once they are created. When a list is created, parentheses are used instead of brackets.

- **Dictionaries**: Dictionaries stored data in key/value pairs. When a dictionary is declared, the data and the key that will point to the data must be specified, and the key-value pairs must be unique. The syntax for creating a key in Python is curly braces containing the key on the left side and the value on the right side, separated by a colon.

- **Inputs**: The input () function gets an input from the user. A string is passed into the parenthesis, which the user will see when they are prompted to enter a string or numerical value.

- **Formatting Printing**: Triple quotes allows us to separate our print statement onto multiple lines. Escape characters are used to specify that certain formatting characters, like "\n" and "\t," should be included in a string's value. Meanwhile, the "raw string" command, "r," can be used to include all the characters within the quotes.

Conclusion

For every programmer, just getting started is always the biggest hurdle. Once you set your mind to things and start writing programs, things automatically start aligning. As you use Python more, it will become automatic.

There is no programmer that I know of personally who can write programs without errors. These errors may be as simple as forgetting to close quotation marks, misplacing a comma, passing the wrong value, and so on. Expect these errors but learn how to avoid them. It takes practice, but there is a good chance you will end up being a programmer who runs into these issues only rarely.

If you have chosen to be a successful Python programmer, know that there will be some extremely fulfilling times ahead. There is nothing like the sense of accomplishment when the program is running properly.

Keep your spirits high and always be ready to encounter failures and mistakes. There is nothing to be ashamed of when going through such things. Instead, look back at your mistakes and learn from them to ensure they are not repeated in the future. You might be able to make programs even better or update the ones which are already functioning well enough.

Lastly, let me say it has been a pleasure to guide you through both these books and to be able to see you convert from a person who had no idea about Python to a programmer who now can code, understand and execute matters at will. Congratulations are in order. Here are digital cheers for you!

> *print ("Bravo, my friend!")*

I wish you the best of luck for your future and hope that one day, you will look back on this book and this experience as a life-changing event that led to a superior success for you as a professional programmer. Do keep an eye out for updates and ensure you visit the forums and other Python communities to gain the finest learning experience and knowledge to serve you even better when stepping into the more advanced parts of Python.

CHAPTER - 2
Python For Data Analysis

Why Python for Data Analysis?

Data Science and Data Analysis

The words of data science and data analytics are often used interchangeably. However, these terms are completely different and have different implications for different businesses. Data science encompasses a variety of scientific models and methods that can be used to manipulate and survey structured, semi-structured, and unstructured data. Tools and processes that can be used to make sense of gather insight from highly complex, unorganized, and raw data set to fall under the category of data science. Unlike data analytics that is targeted to verify a hypothesis, data science boils down to connecting data points to identify new patterns and insights that can be made use of in future planning for the business. Data science moves the business from inquiry to insights by providing a new perspective into their structured and unstructured data by identifying patterns that can allow businesses to increase efficiencies, reduce costs and recognize the new market opportunities.

Data science acts as a multidisciplinary blend of technology, machine learning algorithm development, statistical analysis, and data inference that provides businesses with enhanced capability to solve their most complex business problems. Data analytics falls under the category of data science and pertains more to reviewing and analyzing historical data to put it in context. Unlike data science, data analytics is characterized by low usage of artificial intelligence, predictive modeling, and machine learning algorithms to gather insights from processed and structured data using standard SQL query commands. The seemingly nuanced differences between data analytics and data science can actually have a substantial impact on an organization.

Python as Top Languages for Developers at Top Companies

When startups are planning a process of product development, they need to keep in mind and take note of different factors when it comes to choosing the right language for programming. Moreover, since many startups start from scratch, the budget available is often low, and this is why they very carefully consider factors like how swift the development would be, how popular and widely use the language is factors like the cost of libraries, integrations, and developers. In addition, the cost of security and scalability and not to forget stability. Due to these reasons, it is always preferred by startups around the world and especially in Silicon Valley to opt for a robust and strong technology like Python, which is established and deep-rooted.

This is not the start of technology. It has been around for more than as long as 30 years in the market, and it is so robust and established that it is still one of the tops and best languages for programming that ever existed. This means that Python is so established and widely used that even the latest innovations in the IT sector could not elbow it aside. According to a survey by BuiltWith, as many as one million websites out there are Python customers and have been performing pretty amazingly with great returns. Credit goes to the robust programming language. Another survey about the popularity of Python by TIOBE INDEX reveals that an index called programming community index PCI that measures how popular the programming languages are has ranked Python as the third most famous and popular programming language around the world.

Python for Data Analysis

Python is among the most popular computer language programming tool initially created and designed by Guido Van Rossum in the late 1980s. Since its introduction into the computing world, Python has undergone multiple modifications and improvements, therefore, becoming among leading programming languages used by developers. The tool is dynamically typed, object-oriented, multi-paradigm, and imperative. It is used across different operating systems including Windows, Linux, Android, macOS, and iOS devices. Besides, it is compatible with both bit 32 and bit 64 gadgets of phones, laptops, and desktops.

Despite comprising of several areas essential for programmers, Python is easy to learn, especially when it comes to beginners with minimal knowledge in computer programming. Unlike most programming languages, Python accompanies an easy to use syntaxes where first time users can readily practice and become a pro within a few weeks. However, the programming processes may vary depending on the motive of the learner in programming. Despite accompanying multiple vocabularies and sometimes sophisticated tutorials for learning different programming techniques, engaging with Python is worth it to develop excellent programs.

Data Analysis - The Basics

What Is Data Analysis?

To keep it simple, data analysis is going to be the practice where a company can take their raw data and then order and organize it. When the data is organized in this manner, and run through a predictive model, it is going to help the company extract useful information out of it. The process of organizing and thinking about our data is going to be very important as it is the key to helping us understand what the data does and does not contain at any given time.

Many companies have been collecting data for a long time. They may gather this data from their customers, from surveys, from social media, and many other locations. And while collecting the data is an important step that we need to focus on as well, another thing to consider is what we can do with the data. You can collect all of the data that you would like, but if it just sits in your cloud or a data warehouse and is never mined or used, then it is going to become worthless to you, and you wasted a lot of time and money trying to figure it all out.

This is where data analysis will come in. It is able to take all of that raw data and actually, put it to some good use. It will use various models and algorithms, usually with the help of machine learning and Python, in order to help us to understand what important insights and information are found in our data and how we are able to utilize these for our own benefit.

Why Data Analysis?

While we are here, we need to take a few minutes to discuss why data analysis is so important, and why so many businesses are jumping on board with this in the hopes of seeing some improvements along the way. The reason that data analytics is so important is that it can help a business to optimize its performances overall.

When the company is able to implement the data analysis into their business model, it means that they are able to reduce the costs that they experience on a day to day basis. This happens because the analysis will help them to identify the best, and the most efficient, ways of doing business, and because they are able to store up large amounts of data to help them get all of this process done on time.

Another benefit of using this data analysis, and why it really does matter for a lot of companies, is that the company can use this process to make the best business decisions. These business decisions no longer need to rely on what other companies are doing or on the intuition of key decision-makers. Instead, they rely on the facts and insights provided in the collected data.

Many companies also like to work with the process of data analytics because it will help them learn more about and serve their customers better. Data analytics can help us to analyze customer trends and the satisfaction levels of our customers, which can help the company come up with new, and better, services and products to offer.

Data Analysis Tools

Here are the best tools you can use for data analysis:

- Python
- Xplenty
- IDEA
- Microsoft HDInsight
- Skytree
- Talend
- Splice Machine
- Spark
- Plotly
- Apache SAMOA
- Lumify

Types of Data Analysis: Techniques and Methods

- Text Analysis
- Statistical Analysis
- Descriptive Analysis
- Diagnostic Analysis
- Predictive Analysis

Text Analysis

This is going to be a form of predictive analytics that can help us extract the sentiments behind the text, based on the intensity of the presses on the keys, and the typing speeds.

Statistical Analysis

Statistical analysis involves many aspects of statistics. This analysis uses the concepts in statistics to make certain assumptions and predictions of data that has been collected by a company over a decade. For instance, let us assume that you are a clinical research company, and you have been trying to gather information on certain products being sold by your company. You will conduct thorough research on the type of product, the market you are targeting, and your competitors. Let us assume that you are looking to introduce a painkiller in the market. At such a time, you will try to understand the market better and see what it is that you can offer as compared to the other companies in the market. For you to do this, you will need to conduct a thorough statistical analysis.

Descriptive Analysis

This is a process that is used in data mining and business intelligence. In the descriptive analysis, you will be able to look at data and also analyze the past events. You will be able to obtain insight into approaching the events that may occur in the future. You will use this process to analyze and mine through the data to determine the reasons why the business has either succeeded or failed in the past. Every department in the company would always use this type of analysis to understand their successes and failures.

Diagnostic Analysis

As the name suggests, this type of analysis is done to "diagnose" or understand why a certain event unfolded and how that event can be prevented from occurring in the future or replicated if needed. For example, web marketing strategies and campaigns often employ social media platforms to get publicity and increase their goodwill. Not all campaigns are as successful as expected; therefore, learning from failed campaigns is just as important, if not more. Companies can run diagnostic analysis on their campaign by collecting data about the "social media mentions" of the campaign, number of campaign page views, the average amount of time spent on the campaign page by an individual, number of social media fans and followers of the campaign, online reviews and other related metrics to understand why the campaign failed and how future campaigns can be made more effective.

Predictive Analysis

The predictive analysis gets driven by predictive modeling. It isn't exactly a process but more of an approach. In the case of data science, machine learning, and predictive analysis go hand in hand. The predictive models normally include machine learning algorithms. These models are trained over some time for responding to newer values or data and deliver necessary information for business requirements. Predictive modeling basically overlaps with machine learning.

You can find two kinds of predictive models, and they are classification models and regression models, which predict class membership and numbers, respectively. These models are made up by using algorithms. These algorithms perform statistical analysis and data mining to decide the patterns and trends emerging out of the available data. There are software solutions available for predictive analysis, which comes with built-in algorithms that are utilized for making predictive models. These algorithms are called classifiers, and they identify what set of categories this data belongs to.

Prescriptive Analysis

Prescriptive analysis works towards optimizing and simulating the data and creating a model for the future. This type of analysis helps in synthesizing big data and will also help you understand the rules of business to help you make predictions about the future.

Data Analysis Process

When it comes to working with data analysis, there are going to be a few methods that you are able to work with. These phases will ensure that you can handle the data properly and that it will work the way that we want it to. These are going to include some of the initial phases of cleaning our data, working with whether the data is high enough quality, quality measurement analysis, and then we enter into the main data

analysis.
- Data Requirement Gathering
- Data Collection
- Data Cleaning
- Data Analysis
- Data Interpretation
- Data Visualization

Data Requirement Gathering

It is important to understand what information or data needs to be gathered to meet the business objective and goals. Data organization is also very critical for efficient and accurate data analysis. Some of the categories in which the data can be organized are gender, age, demographics, location, ethnicity, and income. A decision must also be made on the required data types (qualitative and quantitative) and data values (can be numerical or alphanumerical) to be used for the analysis.

Data Collection

It's searching for the data that we want to work with. Once we have a good idea of the information that we need, and the business problem that we would like to solve, it is time for us to go through and look for the data. There are several places where we are able to find this data, such as in surveys, social media, and more, so going out and searching for it here is going to be the best way to gather it up and have it ready to work with on the later steps.

Data Cleaning

The next step that we need to focus on here is data cleaning. While it may not be as much fun as we see with the algorithms and more that come with data analysis, they are still important. This is the part of the process where we match up records, check for multiples and duplicates in the data, and get rid of anything that is false or does not match up with what we are looking for at this time.

Data Analysis

Once the whole process of making sure you clean the data, and we have done the quality analysis and the measurement, it is time to dive into the analysis that we want to use. There are a ton of different analysis that we can do on the information, and it often will depend on what your goals are in this whole process. We can go through and do some graphical techniques that include scattering plots. We can work with some frequency counts to see what percentages and numbers are present. We can do some continuous variables or even the computation of new variables.

Data Interpretation

Look over the insights and hidden patterns that were found in the data. The whole point of working with data analysis is to make sure that we can take a large amount of data and see what important insights are found in that information. The more that we study the data, and the better the algorithm we choose to work with, the easier it is to find the insights and the hidden values that are inside of it. We can then use this to help us make better and more informed decisions.

Data Visualization

This is not a step that you should miss out on at all. These visuals are going to make it easier for those who are in charge of looking over the information to really see the connections and the relationships that show up in that data. This makes it easier for you to really figure out what the data is saying, and to figure out what decisions you should make based on that.

Summarizing the data and what all has happened during the analysis is often going to be pretty important when you would like to support any of the arguments that you made with that data, as is presenting the data in a manner that is clear and understandable. The raw data is something that you may choose to include in the appendix in some cases because this allows those who need it, and why maybe using the information to make important decisions, a way to look through the specifics of the data, of the analysis, and more, if they so choose along the way.

Essential Python Libraries (Numpy, Ipython)

Numpy

NumPy is the key bundle for logical registering in Python. It is a Python library that offers a multidimensional showcase object, unique inferred objects, (for example, veiled clusters and grids), and a grouping of schedules for rapid tasks on clusters, consisting of numerical, coherent, structure control, arranging, choosing, I/O, discrete Fourier changes, quintessential straight variable based math, indispensable factual activities, irregular reenactment and substantially more.

At the heart of the NumPy package is the ndarray object. This exemplifies n-dimensional varieties of homogeneous types of information, with numerous tasks performed when assembling the code for execution. There are some significant contrasts between the well-known NumPy programs and the popular Python groupings.

• NumPy clusters have a constant measurement at creation, distinctive to Python documents (which can advance progressive). Changing the measurement of a ndarray will make some other exhibit and erase the first.

• The aspects in a NumPy cluster are altogether required to be of comparable data type, and in consequence, will be a comparative dimension in memory. The unique case: one can have the sorts of (Python, inclusive of NumPy) objects, alongside these strains taking into account sorts of quite a number estimated components.

• NumPy reveals encourage stepped forward numerical and one of a kind kinds of things to do on massive portions of information. Ordinarily, such duties are carried out more productively and with much fewer code

• Creating lots of logical and scientific Python-based bundles are making use of NumPy exhibits; however, these in most cases bolsters Python-succession input, they convert such contribution to NumPy clusters earlier than preparing, and they frequently yield NumPy clusters. At the end of the day, to efficaciously utilize a great deal (maybe even most) of the present logical/scientific Python-based programming, truly realizing how to make use of Python's labored in succession kinds is missing—one likewise has to realize how to utilize NumPy exhibits.

The focus on grouping size and velocity is particularly widespread in logical registering. As a fundamental model, consider the instance of growing each aspect in a 1-D grouping with the referring to issue in another succession of a comparable length. In the match that the statistics are put away in two Python records, an and b, we should emphasize over each component:

Python Programming

This creates the proper answer, but on the off chance that an and b each comprise a massive number of numbers, we will pay the price for the wasteful elements of circling in Python. We ought to reap a comparable assignment substantially extra swiftly in C through composing (for lucidity, we disregard variable displays and instatements, memory designation, and so forth.)

c = a * b

Does what the preceding fashions do, at shut C speeds, but with the code effortlessness we count on from something dependent on Python. Surely, the NumPy phrase is lots less complex! This last mannequin represents two of NumPy's highlights, which are the premise of a lot of its capacity: vectorization and broadcasting.

Vectorization depicts the non-appearance of any unequivocal circling, ordering, and so forth. In the code—these matters are occurring, obviously, honestly "in the background" in advanced, pre-incorporated C code. Vectorized code has numerous preferences, among which are:

- Vectorized code is steadily brief and less difficult to peruse
- Fewer lines of code for the most section implies fewer bugs
- The code all the extra closely takes after well-known numerical documentation (making it simpler, commonly, to precise code scientific develops)
- Vectorization brings about greater "Pythonic" code. Without vectorization, our code would be covered with wasteful and tough to peruse for circles.

Broadcasting is the term used to depict the sore issue by-component behavior of activities; for the most section talking, in NumPy all tasks, wide variety juggling tasks, yet coherent, piece shrewd, utilitarian, and so forth., elevate on in this verifiable factor by-component design, i.e., they communicate. Besides, in the model over, an and bought to be multidimensional types of a comparable shape, or a scalar and an exhibit, or even two sorts of with a variety of shapes, gave that the little cluster is "expandable" to the kingdom of the higher so that the subsequent talk is unambiguous. For factor by way of point "rules" of broadcasting, see numpy.doc.broadcasting.

Scikit-Learn

You are not going to get too far when it comes to working on a data analysis if you do not bring in the Scikit-Learn library. This is going to be seen as one of the simple and efficient tools that you can use for data mining and for completing data analysis. What is so great about this one is that it is going to be accessible to anyone, and it can be reusable in many contexts as well. It is also going to come to us with a commercially usable license, and it is open source, so we are able to work with it and use it in the manner that we want. Some of the features that we are likely to see with this one includes:

- It can help with problems of classification. This is where it helps us to identify which category a particular object is going to belong with.

- It can help with some problems of regression. This is where it is able to predict a continuous value attribute associated with the object.

- It can help with some problems with clustering. This is where we are going to have an automatic grouping of objects that are similar in the sets.

- It can help us complete something that is known as dimensionality reduction. This is where we can reduce the number of random variables that we want to normalize in all of this.

IPython

Another environment that we can look at is the IPython environment. This is a bit different from some of the others, but it is going to help us to get some more work done. IPython is going to be a shell that is interactive and works well with the Python programming language. It is there to help us to work with many good source codes and can do some tab completion, work with some additional shell syntax, and enhanced introspection all on one.

This is going to be one of the alternatives that we can get with the Python interpreter. A shell is more interactive that can be used for some of the computing that you want to do in Python. Besides, it can provide us with more features based on what we would like to do with our work.

You can enjoy several features when working on the IPython environment. First, it will help you to run more shell commands that are native. When you run any of the interpreters that you would like to use, the interpreter should have several built-in commands. These commands are sometimes going to collide with the native commands of the shell.

For example, if we wanted to work with the traditional interpreter of Python and we typed in the code of "cd" after the interpreter loaded up, you would get an error on your screen. The reason for this error is that the interpreter is not going to recognize this command. This is a command that is native to the terminal of your computer, but not to the Python interpreter. On the other hand, IPython is going to have some more support for those native shell commands so you can utilize them in your work.

IPython is also a good one to work with when it comes to syntax highlighting. One of the first things that we are going to notice about this is that it provides us with syntax highlighting. This means that it is going to use color to help us look over the different parts of the Python code. If you type in $x = 10$ to your terminal, you would be able to see how the IPython environment is going to highlight this code in a variety of colors.

The syntax highlighting is going to be a big improvement over what we see in the default interpreter of Python and can help us to read the code a bit better.

Another benefit of working with IPython is that it works with the proper indentation to help you out. If you have done some coding in the past, you know that it does pay attention to the indentation and whitespace. IPython recognizes this and then automatically provides you with the right indentation as you type the code into this interpreter. This makes things a lot easier as you go through the process.

This environment is also going to work with tab completion. IPython is going to provide us with some tab-completion so that we do not have to worry about handling this. This helps to ensure that the compiler is going to know what is going on with the codes that we write and that all of the work will show up in the manner that you want.

Documentation is another feature that we are able to see with IPython, and it is going to help us to work well with the code. Doing the autocompletion of tabs is going to be useful because it will provide us with a list of all the methods that are possible inside of the specific module. With all of the options at your disposal, you may be confused about what one particular method does. In addition, this is where the documentation of IPython can come into play. It will provide you with the documentation for any method you work with to save time and hassle.

Then the final benefit that we are going to look at here is that IPython can help with pasting blocks of code. IPython is going to be excellent when we want to paste large amounts of Python code. You can grab any block of the Python code, paste it into this environment, and you should get the result of a code that is properly indented and ready to go on this environment. It is as easy as all that.

You can choose to work with the regular Python environment if you would like, but there are also many benefits to upgrading and working with this one as well, especially when you are working with something like data science and completing your own data analysis.

Data Analysis Python Libraries (Matplotlib, Pandas)

What Is Matplotlib?

There are a lot of different libraries that we can work with when it is time to handle visuals and other work of data analysis inside of our Python language. But the library that we are going to spend some time taking a look at is one that is meant to work with the idea of data visualization and why this is so important to some of the work that we want to accomplish.

To start with, you will find that matplotlib is going to be a plotting library that is set up to work with Python. It is also going to be a numerical mathematics extension that works off the arrays that we see in NumPy. This means that if we want to work with the matplotlib library, we need to first make sure that we have NumPy, and sometimes other libraries as well, on our system and ready to go as well.

When we are working with Matplotlib, you will find that it is useful when it is time to provide an API that is object-oriented for embedding plots into applications that will work with some of the toolkits for GUI that is general-purpose. There is also going to be a procedural interface based on a state machine that will work similar to MATLAB, although these are both going to be completely different things from one another, and it is important to work with them differently.

The matplotlib is a great library to work with, and it was originally written by John D. Hunter. It is also going to impress a lot of new programmers because it has an active development community. It is also going to be distributed with a license that is BSD so that it is easier for us to use the way that we would like overall.

There are a lot of really cool options that you can work with when it is time to handle the matplotlib library, and this opens up a lot of opportunities for you when it is time to pick out the different choices in visuals. There are many of these that you are able to work with, and thanks to the way that matplotlib is set up, you will be able to pick out almost any kind of visual that you would like to work with as well.

This means that if you want to make a chart, a pie graph, a bar graph, a histogram, or some other kind of chart, this library is going to have a lot of the additional parts that we are looking for when it is time to handle your data. Make sure to take a look at some of the different options that are provided with this library, and then pay attention to what we are able to do with them before picking the one that is the best for you.

There are also going to be many different toolkits that you can handle when it is time to work with Matplotlib. These toolkits are important because they are going to help us to really extend out the amount of functionality that we will see with this library. Depending on the one that you would like to work with, some of them are going to be separate kinds of downloads, and some are going to ship along with the source code that is found in this library, but their dependencies are going to be found outside of this library, so we have to pay attention to this as well. Some of the different toolkits that we can work with include:

- The basemap: This is going to be a map plotting tool that we can use to help out with different types of projects of a map, coastlines, and political boundaries that we are going to see in here.

• Cartopy: This is another good one to work with when it is time to handle maps and some of that kind of work. This is going to be a mapping library that will have object-oriented map project definitions and arbitrary point lines, image transformation, and even polygon capabilities as well.

• This one can also come with several Excel tools if you would like to work with these as well. This makes it easier for us to use Excel as our database, and you will easily be able to set this up so that you are able to exchange data from your matplotlib library and Excel.

• GTK tools that are going to allow us the ability to interface and work with the GTK+ library if you would like.

• The Qt interface.

• The ability to work with 3-D plots to help out with some of the visuals that you are going to want to use along the way.

• Natgrid: This is going to be an interface that will allow us into the library of natgrid for gridding irregularly spaced data when you would like.

There are a few other libraries that help with visuals if you would like, but we have to remember that this is one of the best ones to work with, and they will keep things as simple and easy to use as possible. And with all of the added and nice features that are going to come with this, you will be able to see some great results with your visuals as well.

Statsmodel

Statsmodel is another Python library for data science widely used for statistical analysis. Statsmodel is a Python library used to perform statistical tests and implement various statistical models for extensive data exploration. Statsmodel was developed at Stanford University by Professor Jonathan Taylor. Compared with Scikit-learn, statsmodel has algorithms for classical statistics and econometrics.

They include submodules such as:

- Regression models such as linear mixed-effects models, robust linear models, generalized linear models, and linear regression.
- Nonparametric methods such as Kernel density estimation and kernel regression.
- Analysis of variance.
- Time series analysis
- Visualization of statistical model results

SciPy

What's SciPy for?

Python customers who prefer a quick and effective math library can use NumPy, however NumPy through itself isn't very task-focused.

How Scipy 1.0 Helps with Data Science

SciPy has always been beneficial for supplying handy and extensively used equipment for working with math and statistics.

The set off for bringing the SciPy challenge to model 1.0, in accordance with core developer Ralf Gommers, used to be specifically a consolidation of how the mission once ran and managed. But it additionally covered a procedure for non-stop integration for the MacOS and Windows builds, as nicely as a suitable aid for prebuilt Windows binaries. This ultimate characteristic ability Windows customers can now use SciPy by not having to soar through extra hoops.

Where to Obtain SciPy?

SciPy binaries can be downloaded from the Python Package Index, or via typing

> *pip install scipy*

Source code is reachable on GitHub.

Pandas

Pandas are going to be a big name when we want to use the Python language to analyze the data we have, and it is actually one of the most used tools that we can bring out when it comes to data wrangling and data munging. Pandas are open-sourced, similar to what we see with some of the other libraries and extensions that are found in Python world. It is also free to use and will be able to handle all of the different parts of your data analysis.

There is a lot that you will enjoy when working with the Pandas library, but one of the neat things is that this library can take data, of almost any format that you would like, and then create a Python object out of it. This is known as a data frame and will have the rows and columns that you need to keep it organized. It is going to look similar to what we are used to seeing with an Excel sheet.

To start with, we are going to use this library to help us to load and save our data. When you want to use this particular library to help out with data analysis, you will find that you can use it in three different manners. These include:

- You can use it to open up a local file with Pandas. This is usually going to be done in a CSV file, but it is also possible to do it in other options like a delimited text file or in Excel.
- You can also open a remote file or a database like JSON or CSV on one of

the websites through a URL, or you can use it to read out the information that is found on an SQL table or database.

Installation and Setup

Installation Instructions for Python

Windows

1. From the official Python website, click on the "Downloads" icon and select Windows.

2. Click on the "Download Python 3.8.0" button to view all the downloadable files.

3. On the subsequent screen, select the Python version you would like to download. We will be using the Python 3 version under "Stable Releases." So scroll down the page and click on the "Download Windows x86-64 executable installer" link.

4. A pop-up window titled "python-3.8.0-amd64.exe" will be shown.

5. Click on the "Save File" button to start downloading the file.

6. Once the download has completed, double click the saved file icon, and a "Python 3.8.0 (64-bit) Setup" pop window will be shown.

7. Make sure that you select the "Install Launcher for all users (recommended)" and the "Add Python 3.8 to PATH" checkboxes. Note—If you already have an older version of Python installed on your system, the "Upgrade Now" button will appear instead of the "Install Now" button, and neither of the checkboxes will be shown.

8. Click on "Install Now" and a "User Account Control" pop up window will be

Python Programming

shown.

9. A notification stating, "Do you want to allow this app to make changes to your device" will be shown, click on Yes.

10. A new pop up window titled "Python 3.8.0 (64-bit) Setup" will be shown containing a setup progress bar.

11. Once the installation has been completed, a "Set was successful" message will be shown. Click on Close.

12. To verify the installation, navigate to the directory where you installed Python and double click on the python.exe file.

Macintosh

1. From the official Python website, click on the "Downloads" icon and select Mac.

2. Click on the "Download Python 3.8.0" button to view all the downloadable files.

3. On the subsequent screen, select the Python version you would like to download. We will be using the Python 3 version under "Stable Releases." So scroll down the page and click on the "Download macOS 64-bit installer" link under Python 3.8.0, as shown in the picture below.

4. A pop-up window titled "python-3.8.0-macosx10.9.pkg" will be shown.

5. Click "Save File" to start downloading the file.

6. Once the download has completed, double click the saved file icon, and an "Install Python" pop window will be shown.

7. Click "Continue" to proceed, and the terms and conditions pop up window will appear.

8. Click Agree and then click "Install."

9. A notification requesting administrator permission and password will be shown. Enter your system password to start the installation.

10. Once the installation has finished, an "Installation was successful" message will appear. Click on the Close button, and you are all set.

11. To verify the installation, navigate to the directory where you installed Python and double click on the python launcher icon that will take you to the Python Terminal.

Getting Started

With the Python terminal installed on your computer, you can now start writing and executing the Python code. All Python codes are written in a text editor as (.py) files and executed on the Python interpreter command line as shown in the code below, where "nineplanets.py" is the name of the Python file:

"C: \Users\Your Name\python nineplanets.py"

You will be able to test a small code without writing it in a file and simply executing it as a command line itself by typing the code below on the Mac, Windows, or Linux command line, as shown below:

"C: \Users\Your Name\python"

In case the command above does not work, use the code below instead:

"C: \Users\Your Name\py"

Indentation – The importance of indentation, which is the number of spaces preceding the code, is fundamental to the Python coding structure. In most programming languages, indentation is added to enhance the readability of the code. However, in Python, the indentation is used to indicate the execution of a subset of the code, as shown in the code below

```
if 7 > 2:
    print ('Seven is greater than two')
```

Indentation precedes the second line of code with the print command. If the indentation is skipped and the code was written as below, an error will be triggered:

> *if 7 > 2:*
> *print ('Seven is greater than two')*

The number of spaces can be modified but is required to have at least one space. For example, you can execute the code below with higher indentation, but for a specific set of codes, the same number of spaces must be used, or you will receive an error.

Adding Comments

> In Python, comments can be added to the code by starting the code comment lines with a "#," as shown in the example below: if 7 > 2:
> *print ('Seven is greater than two')*
> *#Any relevant comments will be added here*
> *print ('Nine planets')*

Comments serve as a description of the code and will not be executed by the Python terminal. Make sure to remember that any comments at the end of the code line will lead to the entire code line being skipped by the Python terminal, as shown in the code below. Comments can be very useful in case you need to stop the execution when you are testing the code.

Python Variables

> In Python, variables are primarily utilized to save data values without executing a command for it. A variable can be created by simply assigning the desired value to it, as shown in the example below: A = 999
> *B = 'Patricia'*
> *print (A)*
> *print (B)*

A variable could be declared without a specific data type. The data type of a variable can also be modified after it's an initial declaration, as shown in the example below:

> *A = 999 # A has data type set as int*
> *A = 'Patricia' # A now has data type str*
> *print (A)*

Some of the rules applied to the Python variable names are as follows:

- Variable names could be as short as single alphabets or more descriptive words like height, weight, and more.

- Variable names could only be started with an underscore character or a letter.

- Variable names must not start with numbers.

- Variable names can contain underscores or alphanumeric characters. No other special characters are allowed.

- Variable names are case sensitive. For example, 'weight,' 'Weight,' and 'WEIGHT' will be accounted for as 3 separate variables.

Assigning Value to Variables

In Python, multiple variables can be assigned DISTINCT values in a single code line, as shown in the example below:

Python Programming

> A, B, C = 'violet', 'maroon', 'teal'
> print (A)
> print (B)
> print (C)

To view the data type of any object, you can use the "type ()" function as shown in the example below:

> A = 'Violet'
> print (type (A))

Assigning the Data Type to Variables

A new variable can be created by simply declaring a value for it. This set data value will, in turn, assign the data type to the variable.

To assign a specific data type to a variable, the constructor functions listed below are used:

Constructor Functions	Data Type
A = str ('Nine Planets)'	str
A = int (55)	Int (Must be a whole number, positive or negative, with no decimals, no length restrictions)

A = float (14e6)	Float (Floating point number must be a positive or negative number with one or more decimals; maybe scientific number an 'e' to specify an exponential power of 10)
A = complex (92j)	Complex (Must be written with a 'j' as an imaginary character)
A = list ['teal', maroon, 'jade']	list
A = range (3, 110)	range
A = tuple ('teal', maroon, 'jade')	tuple
A = set {'teal', maroon, 'jade'}	set
A = frozenset ({ 'teal', 'jade', maroon})	frozenset
A = dict ('color' : maroon, 'year' : 1988)	dict
A = bool (False)	bool
A = bytes (542)	bytes
A = bytearray (9)	bytearray
A = memoryview (bytes (525))	memoryview

EXERCISE – To solidify your understanding of data types; look at the first column of the table below and write the data type for that variable. Once you have all your answers, look at the second column, and verify your answers.

Python Programming

Variable	Data Type
A = 'Nine Planets'	str
A = 45	int
A = 56e2	float
A = 34j	complex
A = ['teal', maroon, 'jade']	list
A = range (12, 103)	range
A = ('teal', maroon, 'jade')	tuple
A = {'teal', maroon, 'jade'}	set
A = frozenset ({ 'teal', 'jade', maroon})	frozenset
A = ['color' : maroon, 'year' : 1939}	dict
A = False	bool
A = b 'Morning'	bytes
A = bytearray (5)	bytearray
A = memoryview (bytes (45))	memoryview

Output Variables

In order to retrieve variables as output, the "print" statements are used in Python. You can use the "+" character to combine text with a variable for final output, as shown in the example below:

> *A = "maroon"*
> *print ("Flowers are" + A)*

OUTPUT – 'Flowers are maroon'

A variable can also be combined with another variable using the "+" character as shown in the example below:

```
A = "Flowers are"
B = "maroon"
AB = A + B
print (AB)
```

OUTPUT – "Flowers are maroon'"

However, when the "+" character is used with numeric values, it retains its function as a mathematical operator, as shown in the example below:

```
A = 22
B = 33
print (A + B)
```

OUTPUT = 55

You will not be able to combine a string of characters with numbers and will trigger an error instead, as shown in the example below:

```
A = "yellow"
B = 30
print (A + B)
```

OUTPUT – N/A – ERROR

Specific steps and instructions are followed to download and install Python on your operating system by referring to the relevant section. The latest version of Python released in the middle of 2019 is Python 3.8.0 is preferred. Make sure to download and install the most recent and stable version of Python at the time of installation.

Python Language Basics, IPython and Jupyter Notebooks

IPython

IPython, same as Interactive Python, is a capable toolkit that allows you to experience Python interactively. It has two main components: a dependent Python Shell interface, and Jupyter kernels.

These components have many features, such as:
- Persistent input history
- Caching of outputs
- Code completition
- Support for 'magic' commands
- Highly customizable settings
- Syntax highlighting
- Session logging
- Access to system Shell
- Support to python's debugger and profiler

Now, let's go into each of these components and see how these features come to life.

IPython Shell

The objective of this Shell is to provide a superior experience than the default Python REPL.

To run the IPython Shell, you just need to call the command bellow on your system console.

§ Interface

At first glance, the IPython Shell looks like a normal boring Shell, with some initial version information, and some user tips. However, it has great features that make it shine.

§ Help

You can type "?" after an accessible object at any time you want more details about it.

§ Code Completition

You can press "TAB" key at any time to trigger the code completition.

§ Syntax Highlight

The code is automatically highlighted depending on the variables and keywords you are using.

§ Run External Commands

External commands can be run directly using "!" at the beginning of the input.

§ Magic Commands

Magic commands add incredible capabilities to IPython. Some commands are shown below:

%time – Shows the time to execute the command.

%timeit – Shows the mean and standard deviation of the time to execute the command.

%pdb – Run the code in debug mode, creating breakpoints on uncaught exceptions.

%matplotlib – This command arranges all the setup needed to IPython work correctly with matplotlib, this way IPython can display plots that are outputs of running code in new windows.

There are multiple magic commands that be used on IPython Shell, for a full list of the built-in commands check this link or type "%lsmagic".

Jupiter Notebook

Getting Started with Jupyter Notebook (Ipython)

The Jupyter Note pad is an open-source web application that permits you to produce and share files that contain live code, formulas, visualizations, and narrative text. Utilizes consist of information cleansing and change, mathematical simulation, analytical modeling, information visualization, artificial intelligence, and far more.

Jupyter has assistance for over 40 various shows languages, and Python is among them. Python is a requirement (Python 3.3 or higher, or Python 2.7) for setting up the Jupyter Notebook itself.

Setting Up Jupyter Utilizing Anaconda

Set up Python and Jupyter utilizing the Anaconda Distribution, which includes Python, the Jupyter Notebook, and other typically utilized bundles for clinical computing and information science. You can download Anaconda's newest Python3 variation.

Command to Run the Jupyter Notebook

When the Notepad opens in your Internet browser, you will see the Notebook Dashboard, which will reveal a list of the notepads, files, and subdirectories in the directory site where the Notepad server was started. Most of the time, you will want to begin a Notepad server in the greatest level directory site consisting of notepads. Typically, this will be your house directory site.

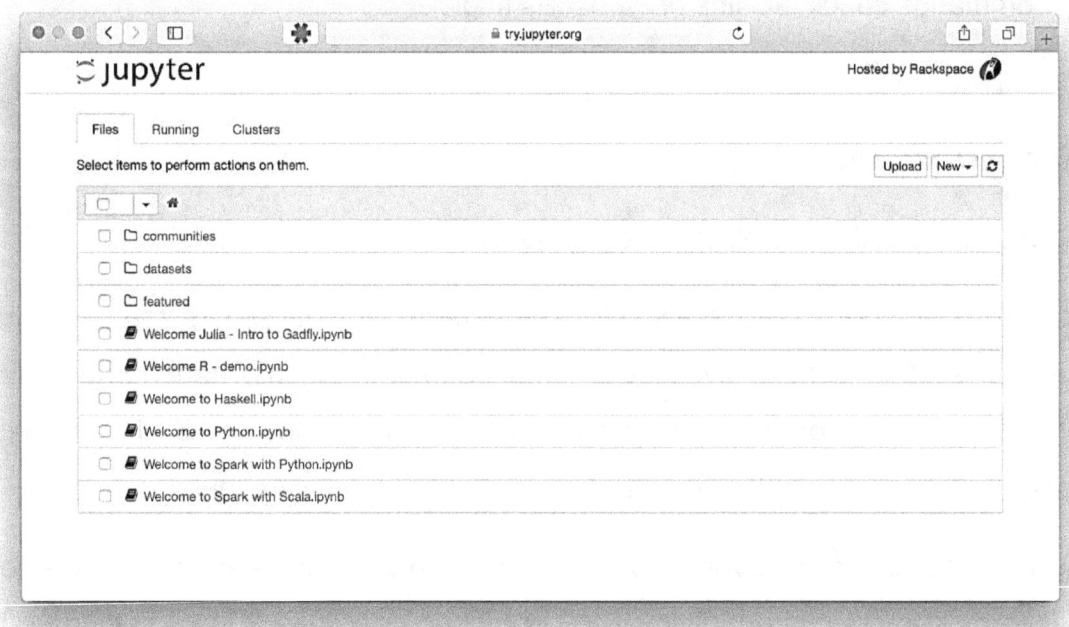

Built-in Data Structures, Functions, and Files

Python Data Structures – Lists, Tuples, Sets, Dictionaries

Data structure is a way to organize and store data where we can access and modify it efficiently.

Let's begin with our first Python Data Structures and lists.

Python List

We create a list in Python by placing items called elements inside square brackets separated by commas. The items in a list can be of mixed data types.

Start IDLE.

Navigate to the File menu and click New Window.

Type the following:

```
list_mine=[] #empty list
list_mine=[2,5,8] #list of integers
list_mine=[5,"Happy", 5.2] #list having mixed data types
```

How to Declare Python List?

Just input:

\>\>\> languages=['C++','Python','Scratch']

You can put any kind of value in a list.

\>\>\> list1=[1,[2,3],(4,5),False,'No']

How to Access Python List?

In Python, the first time is always indexed as zero. A list of five items can be accessed by index0 to index4. An index error will occur if you fail to access the items in a list.

The index is always an integer, so using other numbers will also create a type error.

Example

Start IDLE.

Navigate to the File menu and click New Window.

Type the following:

> *list_mine=['b','e','s','t']*
> *print(list_mine[0])#the output will be b*
> *print(list_mine[2])#the output will be s*
> *print(list_mine[3])#the output will be t*

Slicing a Python List

Slicing operator (full colon) is used to access a range of elements in a list.

Example

Start IDLE.

Navigate to the File menu and click New Window.

Type the following:

> *list_mine=['c','h','a','n','g','e','s']*
> *print(list_mine[3:5]) #Picking elements from the fourth to the sixth*

A List Is Mutable

Items in a list can be changed, meaning lists are mutable.

Start IDLE.

Navigate to the File menu and click New Window.

Type the following:

```
list_yours=[4,8,5,2,1]
list_yours[1]=6
print(list_yours) #The output will be [4,6,5,2,1]
```

How to Delete a Python List?

The keyword del is used to delete elements or the entire list in Python.

Example

Start IDLE.

Navigate to the File menu and click New Window.

Type the following:

```
list_mine=['t','r','o','g','r','a','m']
del list_mine[1]
print(list_mine) #t, o, g, r, a, m
```

Reassigning a List in Python

Create a new list and then reassign on it.

>>> list1=[1,2,3,4,5,6,7,8]

To reassign a single item:

>>> list1[0]=0

>>> list1

[0, 2, 3, 4, 5, 6, 7, 8]

To reassign a slice:

```
>>> list1[1:3]=[9,10,11]

>>> list1

[0, 9, 10, 11, 4, 5, 6, 7, 8]
```

To reassign the entire list

Finally, let's reassign the entire list.

```
>>> list1=[0,0,0]

>>> list1

[0, 0, 0]
```

Python Tuple

In Python, Tuples are collections of data types that cannot be changed but can be arranged in specific order. Tuples allow for duplicate items and are written within round brackets, as shown in the syntax below.

> *Tuple = ("string001", "string002", "string003")*
> *print (Tuple)*

Similar to the Python List, you can selectively display the desired string from a Tuple by referencing the position of that string inside square bracket in the print command as shown below.

> *Tuple = ("string001", "string002", "string003")*
> *print (Tuple [1])*

OUTPUT – *("string002")*

Python Programming

Python Tuple Packing

Here's how to pack values into a tuple

>>> mytuple=1,2,3, #Or it could have been mytuple=1,2,3

>>> mytuple

Python Tuple Unpacking

Here's how unpack values from tuple

>>> a,b,c=mytuple

>>> print(a,b,c)

Creating a Tuple with a Single Item

Make a tuple and assign 0 to it.

>>> a=(0)

Then, call the type() function on it.

>>> type(a)

<class 'int'>

As you can see, this declared an integer, not a tuple.

Then, you need to append a comma to the end of the first item 0. This tells the interpreter that it's a tuple.

>>> a=(0,)

>>> type(a)

<class 'tuple'>

Accessing, Reassigning, and Deleting Items

You can access Python Tuple with the same operations from Python Lists

Unlike Python lists, you cannot directly change the data value of Python Tuples after they have been created. However, conversion of a Tuple into a List and then modifying the data value of that List will allow you to subsequently create a Tuple from that updated List. Let's look at the example below:

Tuple1 = ("string001", "string002", "string003", "string004", "string005", "string006")
List1 = list (Tuple1)
List1 [2] = "update this list to create new tuple"
Tuple1 = tuple (List1)
print (Tuple1)

OUTPUT – ("string001", "string002", "update this list to create new tuple", "string004", "string005", "string006")

You can also determine the length of a Python Tuple using the "len()" function, as shown in the example below:

Tuple = ("string001", "string002", "string003", "string004", "string005", "string006")
print (len (Tuple))

OUTPUT – 6

You cannot selectively delete items from a Tuple, but you can use the "del" keyword to delete the Tuple in its entirety, as shown in the example below:

Tuple = ("string001", "string002", "string003", "string004")
del Tuple
print (Tuple)

OUTPUT – name 'Tuple' is not defined

> You can join multiple Tuples with the use of the "+" logical operator. Tuple1 = ("string001", "string002", "string003", "string004")
>
> *Tuple2 = (100, 200, 300)*
>
> *Tuple3 = Tuple1 + Tuple2*
>
> *print (Tuple3)*

OUTPUT – ("string001", "string002", "string003", "string004", 100, 200, 300)

You can also use the "tuple ( )" constructor to create a Tuple, as shown in the example below:

> *Tuple1 = tuple (("string001", "string002", "string003", "string004"))*
> *print (Tuple1)*

Python Set

In Python, sets are collections of data types that cannot be organized and indexed. Sets do not allow for duplicate items and must be written within curly brackets, as shown in the syntax below:

> *set = {"string1", "string2", "string3"}*
> *print (set)*

Unlike the Python List and Tuple, you cannot selectively display desired items from a Set by referencing the position of that item because the Python Set are not arranged in any order.

Unlike Python Lists, you cannot directly change the data values of Python Sets after they have been created. However, you can use the "add ()" method to add a single item to Set and use the "update ( )" method to one or more items to an already existing Set. Let's look at the example below:

> *set = {"string1", "string2", "string3"}*
> *set. add ("newstring")*
> *print (set)*

OUTPUT – *{"string1", "string2", "string3", "newstring"}*

> *set = {"string1", "string2", "string3"}*
> *set. update (["newstring1", "newstring2", "newstring3",)*
> *print (set)*

OUTPUT – *{"string1", "string2", "string3", "newstring1", "newstring2", "newstring3"}*

Python Dictionaries

Python dictionary is used to store data by using a unique key for each entry. Key is somehow serving the same functionality as indices in lists and tuples when we want to refer to a certain element. The values where each key refers to are not necessarily unique. Dictionaries are mutable, so we can add, delete, or modify the elements in it.

The entries of a dictionary are contained between curly braces {}. Each entry is in the form key: value.

Now that we have everything set up, we can start to get used to the programming language. Here we present the basic concepts of Python, from variable declaration to the principles of the language.

Therefore, we go into details about the basic syntax, flow control blocks, and intrinsic peculiarities. All these topics work as a presentation to the language for new users, or as a reminder for readers with good knowledge.

NumPy Basics: Arrays and Vectorized Computation

What Is a Python NumPy Array?

NumPy is one of the fundamental packages that are out there when you want to use Python to do scientific computing. It is going to be a Python library that you can choose to use because it will provide you with a lot of different things that make scientific computing a little bit easier to work with. First, it is going to provide you with an array of objects that are seen as multidimensional. Then it is able to provide us with various objects that are derived, which could include matrices and masked arrays. And then, there is an assortment of routines that are used for making the operation on the array that much faster.

Another thing to consider is that the arrays that come with NumPy are going to be able to help out with some more of the advanced mathematical options that you can do, including operations that are meant to work on large numbers of data at the same time. While it is possible to do this with the Python sequence if you choose, it is going to take a lot less code and will be more efficient to rely on the arrays from NumPy instead.

How to Install NumPy

Installing NumPy on a Mac OS

The first operating system that we will look at is how to install the NumPy on our Mac computers. We can do this with several different Python versions, and the steps are similar to one another to make things easier. To start, we need to open up the terminal on your computer. Also, you get that open, type in python to get the prompt for this language to open for you. When you get to this part, follow the steps below to help get it going:

We want to press on Command and then the Space Bar. This will help us to open up the spotlight search. Type in the word "Terminal" before pressing on entering.

This should bring up the terminal that we want to use. We can then use the command of pip in order to install the NumPy package. This requires the coding of "pip install numpy" to get going.

Once you have gotten a successful install, you can type in python to this again to get that python prompt. You should check to see which version of python is displayed there. You can then choose to use your command of import to include the package of NumPy and use it in any codes that you would like in the future.

That method works the best with Python 2.7. You can also go through and install the NumPy package on Python 3. This is going to be similar. However, when you are done opening the terminal that we detailed in the first step above, you would use the pip3 command in order to install NumPy. Notice that we are going to work with pip3 rather than pip from before. Otherwise, the steps are going to be the same.

Installing NumPy on a Windows System

It is important to remember that the Python language is not going to be on the Windows operating system by default, so we need to go through and do the installation on our own to use it. You can go to www.python.org and find the version that you want to use. Follow the steps that are there to get Python ready to go on your own computer. Once you have been able to get Python installed successfully, you can then open up the command prompt that is on your computer and use pip in order to install the NumPy library.

How to Make NumPy Arrays

From here, we need to take some time to learn how to create these arrays. We will assume that you already have the NumPy library on your computer and ready to go. There are then two main ways that we are able to create some of these arrays, including:

You can go through and make one of these arrays with the nested list or the Python list.

We can also work with some of the methods that are built-in with NumPy to make these arrays.

We are going to start out by looking at the steps that are necessary in order to create an array from the nested list and the Python list. To do this, we just need to pass the list from Python with the method of np.array() as your argument, and then you are done. When you do this, you will get either a vector or a 1D array, which can help you to get a lot of the necessary work done.

There are also times when we want to take this a bit further. We would want to get out of the 1D array that we just created, and we want to turn it into a 2D array or a matrix. To do this, we simply need to pass the Python list of lists to the method of np.array(), and then it is done for us.

How NumPy Broadcasting Works

Broadcasting refers to the ability of NumPy to perform arithmetic operations on different shaped arrays. If two arrays have the same shape, then arithmetic operations are easily performed since they are between corresponding elements. This becomes impossible in the case of differently sized arrays, but NumPy has a solution for this. In NumPy, the smaller array is "broadcasted" across the larger array so that they have the same shapes. It will be clear by this example:

Suppose I have an array 'A' of 4X5 shape and an array 'B' of size 1X5, then the smaller array B is stretched such that it also has a size of 4X5, same as 'A.' The new elements in B are simply a copy of original elements.

1	71	8	5	0
7	4	35	8	11
62	0	4	14	2
2	15	86	13	10

Array A

1	3	2	1	5
1	3	2	1	5
1	3	2	1	5
1	3	2	1	5

Array B

2	74	10	6	5
8	7	37	9	16
63	3	6	15	7
3	18	88	14	15

Array A+b

Note: NumPy doesn't actually make copies of elements, instead it uses the original scalar value repeatedly to make it as memory and computationally efficient as possible.

How Do Array Mathematics Work?

NumPy supports easy computation of various functions, including mathematical, binary, statistical, and trigonometry.

Mathematical functions:

There are 2 types of functions:

1) Unary: that require only 1 operator

2) Binary: that requires 2 operators

NumPy has special keywords that let you perform both these operations without explicitly defining the machine what these functions do, for example:

- Addition: np.add(arr1,arr2). It Add corresponding elements of 2 arrays.

- Subtract: np.subtract(arr1,arr2). It Subtract elements of second array from first array.

- Multiply: np.multiply(arr1,arr2) or np.multiply(arr1, 5). It multiplies corresponding array elements. It can also be done by multiplying the whole array with a scaler value.

- divide, floor_divide: Divide gives you complete value including remainder while floor divide truncates the remainder and only returns the integer part

- Power : np.power(arr1,arr2). Raise elements in the first array to powers indicated in the second array. you can also specify the same power of all by writing arr1 ** 2

- Modulus: np.mod(arr1, arr2) finds Element-wise modulus i.e remainder of division

- Logical operators: greater, greater_equal, less, less_equal, equal, not_equal, logical_and, logical_or, logical_xor , all Perform element-wise comparison, and giving result in terms of boolean array .

How to Slice, and Index Arrays

Sometimes you need only a subset of your data or need the value of some individual elements. Then you can do this by indexing and slicing. This is the way to address individual elements. One important thing to remember is that indexing always starts with '0.' For a single-dimensional matrix, indexing is pretty easy.

Syntax for indexing in 1 dimensional matrix is given as arr[n], this gives you nth number starting with zero index.

For a 2-dimensional matrix, you can pass a comma-separated list of indices to select individual elements. It is given as arr[m,n] or arr[m][n], this gives you the element on mth row and nth column starting with zero index.

	0	1	2
0	(0,0)	(0,1)	(0,2)
1	(1,0)	(1,1)	(1,2)
2	(2,0)	(2,1)	(2,2)

Now when we talk about indexing in the multidimensional matrix, it becomes a little more difficult. Multidimensional matrix is basically a list of the list with multiple layers.

Here I am going to talk about a 3-dimensional matrix. Indexing in a 3d array works like this: syntax: arr[L,M,N] or arr [L][M][N] where L is the first index, M is the row no. and N is the column no.

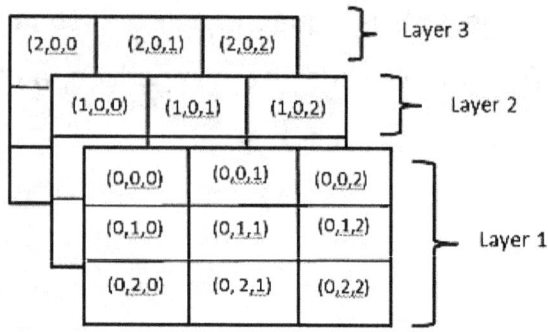

If you omit later indices in multidimensional arrays, then all data along higher dimension will be returned; for example, in a 3d array, if we search for arr[3] it returns all the elements of layer 3.

All this is shown in example below:

```
>>> Array1= np.array([1, 2, 3, 4, 5, 6])

Array1[5]

6

>>> Array1=Array1.reshape(2,3)

>>> Array1[0,1]

2

>>>array3d =np.array([ [[1, 2, 5],[6,0,2]] , [[5,9,8],[0,3,2]] ])

>>> array1[1,0,1]

9

>>> array1[1]

array([[5, 9, 8]

[0, 3, 2]])
```

Slicing on the other hand is basically an operation that is used mainly to select a subset of an existing array. Continues values can be selected separated by colon (:). In all these cases the returned array are views. Views are basically virtual table that shows most recent data. However, it doesn't store the data. This means that the data is not copied, and any modifications will be reflected in the source array. So it's better to create a copy of that array if you feel like you will be needing the original data later.

Slicing in 1-D array: arr[x : y] , It returns all the elements indexed from x to (y-1) .

In multidimensional arrays you can address it using rows and columns to include. It will be more clear to understand by visualizing it in this way:

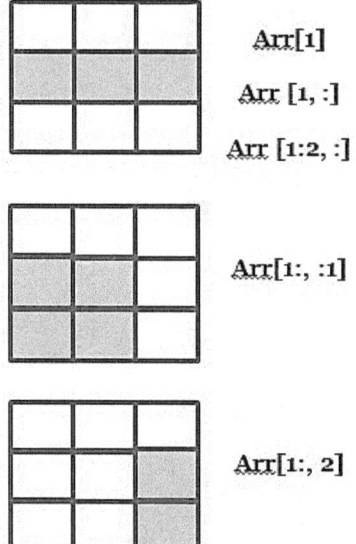

How to Ask for Help

There are two ways to ask for help in Numpy:

- Use look for() to do a keyword search on docstrings.
- Use info() for quick explanations and code examples of functions, classes, or modules. How to Manipulate Arrays.

Appending to Arrays

IPYTHON SHELL:

```
>>> ar = np.arange(5)          # Values from 0 to 5
                                 with step 1
>>> ar2 = np.append(ar, 5)     # New array with
                                 value appended
array([0, 1, 2, 3, 4, 5])

>>> ar3 = np.append(ar, [5, 6]) # New array with
                                  values appended
array([0, 1, 2, 3, 4, 5, 6])

>>> ar
array([0, 1, 2, 3, 4])
```

Differently from lists, numpy arrays have fixed sizes. Therefore, to append a value in the array, a new array is created, and the values are copied. This can be done with the append function, which accepts values or other arrays. For large arrays, this is a costly operation and should be avoided. A good practice is to create the array with extra spaces and fill it.

Stacking and Concatenating Arrays

There are several functions that can perform the combinations of arrays, such as hstack and vstack. These functions are easily understandable when applied to arrays up to three dimensions. For more dimensions, the general functions stack and concatenate are more appropriate.

```
IPYTHON SHELL:
>>> ar1 = np.zeros((2,2))        # 2x2 with 0s
>>> ar2 = np.ones((2,2))         # 2x2 with 1s
>>> np.vstack((ar1, ar2))        # Combine on first axis
array([[0., 0.],
       [0., 0.],
       [1., 1.],
       [1., 1.]])

>>> np.hstack((ar1, ar2))        # Combine on second axis
array([[0., 0., 1., 1.],
       [0., 0., 1., 1.]])

>>> np.concatenate((ar3, ar2), axis=1)
                                 # Equivalent to hstack
array([[1., 1., 0., 0.],
       [1., 1., 0., 0.]])

>>> ar4 = np.stack((ar2, ar1))   # Created new dimension
>>> ar4
array([[[1., 1.],
        [1., 1.]],

       [[0., 0.],
        [0., 0.]]])
>>> ar4.shape
(2, 2, 2)
```

How to Visualize NumPy Arrays

Visualizing Numpy Arrays using np.histogram()

First, you input the data or the array that you are working with.

Python Programming

```python
# Import `numpy` as `np`
import numpy as np

# Initialize your array
my_3d_array = np.array([[[1,2,3,4], [5,6,7,8]], [[1,2,3
,4], [9,10,11,12]]], dtype=np.int64)

# Pass the array to `np.histogram()`
print(np.histogram(my_3d_array))

# Specify the number of bins
print(np.histogram(my_3d_array, bins=range(0,13)))
```

Then the histogram will be computed.

To visualize the data or array, you need the help of Matplotlib, plt.hist() will do it for itself when you pass the data and the bins.

```python
# Import numpy and matplotlib
import numpy as np
import matplotlib.pyplot as plt

# Construct the histogram with a flattened 3d array and a range of bins
plt.hist(my_3d_array.ravel(), bins=range(0,13))

# Add a title to the plot
plt.title('Frequency of My 3D Array Elements')

# Show the plot
plt.show()
```

Then the code above will give you this histogram:

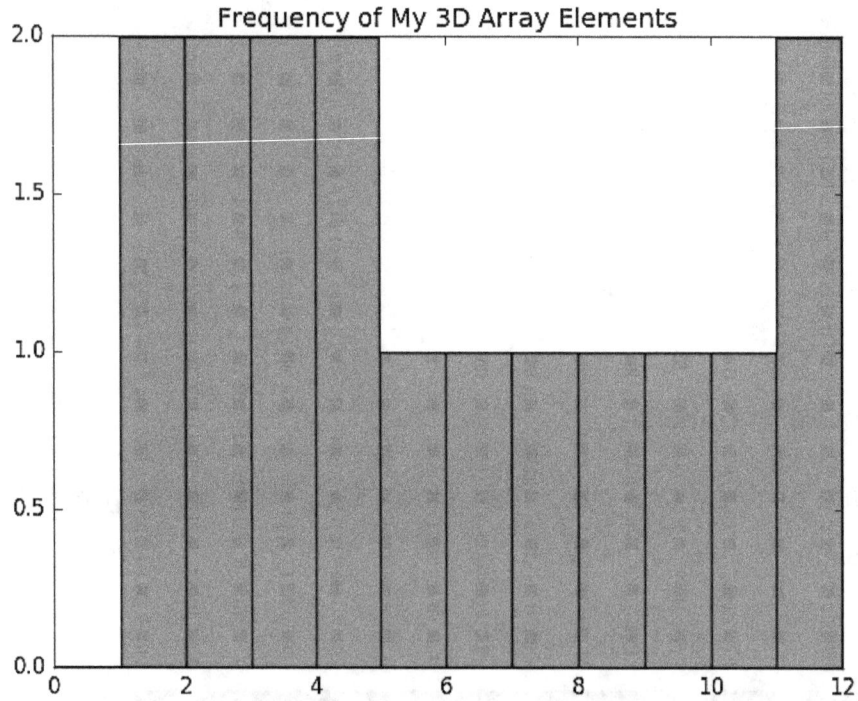

Beyond Data Analysis with NumPy

Now that we have had some time to explore other languages and some of the reasons why you would want to work with this kind of library in addition to the regular library that is available through Python, it is time to take a look at a second library that can be really useful as well. And for this library, we talked about NumPy.

Getting Started with Pandas

Pandas Installation

For installing Python Pandas, you need to go to the command line or terminal and then type "pip install pandas." Otherwise, in case you have anaconda installed on your computer, you may type in "conda install pandas." When this installation is finished, go to the IDE, which may be PyCharm or Jupyter, and just import it with the command, "import pandas as pd." By moving forward with Python Pandas topic, let us take a closer look at some of the operations it performs.

Basic Structures in Pandas

With some of this in mind, it is time for us to go through a few of the different things that we can do with the Pandas code. First, we need to look at the data structures. There are two of these data structures that we can work with, including the series and the DataFrame.

The first one here is the series. This is going to be similar to what we can work with when it comes to a one-dimensional array. It is able to go through and store data of any type. The values of a Pandas Series are going to be mutable, but you will find that the size of our series is going to be immutable, and we are not able to change them later.

The first element in this series is going to be given an index of 0. Then the last element that is going to be found in this kind of index is N-1 because N is going to be the total number of elements that we put into our series. To create one of our own Series in Pandas, we need to first go through the process of importing the package of Pandas through the insert command of Python. The code that we can use, including:

Import pandas as pd

Then we can go through and create one of our own Series. We are going to invoke the method of pd.Series() and then pass on the array. This is simple to work with. The code that we are able to use to help us work with this includes:

Series1 = pd.Series([1, 2, 3, 4])

We need to then work with the print statement to display the contents of the Series. You can see that when you run this one, you have two columns. The first one is going to be the first one with numbers starting from the index of 0 like we talked about before, and then the second one is going to be the different elements that we added to our series. The first column is going to denote the indexes for the elements.

However, you could end up with an error if you are working with the display Series. The major cause of this error is that the Pandas library is going to take some time to look for the amount of information that is displayed, this means that you need to provide the sys output information. You are also able to go through this with the help of a NumPy array like we talked about earlier. This is why we need to make sure that when we are working with the Pandas library, we also go through and install and use the NumPy library as well.

The second type of data structure that we can work with here will include the DataFrames. These are going to often come in as a table. It is going to be able to organize the data into columns and rows, which is going to turn it into a two-dimensional data structure. This means that we have the potential to have columns that are of a different type, and the size of the DataFrame that we want to work with will be mutable, and then it can be modified.

To help us to work with this and create one of our own, we need to either go through and start out a new one from scratch, or we are going to convert other data structures, like the arrays for NumPy into the DataFrame.

Pandas DataFrame

A Pandas DataFrame is probably the most used data structure offered by Pandas. A Pandas DataFrame is a rectangular table that contains an ordered collection of columns. A DataFrame column can each consist of different data types such as Booleans, strings, integers, etc. Unlike a series, a Pandas DataFrame has both rows and column indices. The best way to think of a Pandas as a DataFrame is like a spreadsheet document, or, on a more technical side, a dictionary of Pandas series sharing a unique index.

The most common way to create a Pandas DataFrame is by passing a python dictionary that contains equal length lists or a Numpy array to the DataFrame function.

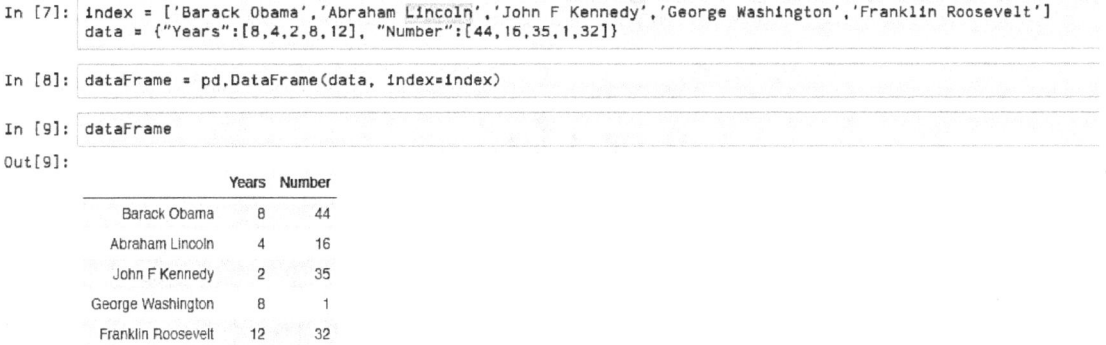

First, we create a list containing the most popular presidents in the USA. Next, we create a dictionary containing their service years and the number in which they served as president. Finally, we pass the data to the DataFrame function and their names as the index for the data. That results in a data frame containing the names of the presidents as the index, their service years as column 1, and their service number as column 2.

NOTE: Use Jupyter notebook while working with DataFrames as the formatting is friendly—HTML.

To retrieve a column in a Pandas DataFrame, we use either the dictionary notation—where we use the column name by using the attribute.

```
In [22]: dataFrame['Presidents']
Out[22]: 0         Barack Obama
         1      Abraham Lincoln
         2       John F Kennedy
         3    George Washington
         4    Franklin Roosevelt
         Name: Presidents, dtype: object
```

```
In [24]: dataFrame.Presidents
Out[24]: 0         Barack Obama
         1      Abraham Lincoln
         2       John F Kennedy
         3    George Washington
         4    Franklin Roosevelt
         Name: Presidents, dtype: object
```

Note that retrieving a column from a Pandas DataFrame produces a Pandas Series with its unique indices. This shows that a Pandas DataFrame consists of many Pandas Series. If you call the type function off the column, you will get a Pandas.core.series.Series data type.

Python Programming

```
In [25]: type(dataFrame.Presidents)
Out[25]: pandas.core.series.Series
```

We can also retrieve the rows of a Pandas DataFrame using a special loc attribute.

```
In [16]: dataFrame.loc['Abraham Lincoln']
Out[16]: Years     4
         Number   16
         Name: Abraham Lincoln, dtype: int64
```

NOTE: Depending on the method you use to execute the code used in the book, you might need to use the row number instead of the president's name and vice versa.

You can modify the Pandas dataframe columns by creating new ones and adding values to them. Let us add state column in our President's DataFrame as shown:

```
In [18]: dataFrame['State'] = ['Hawaii','Kentucky','Massachusetts','Virginia','New
```

```
In [19]: dataFrame
Out[19]:
```

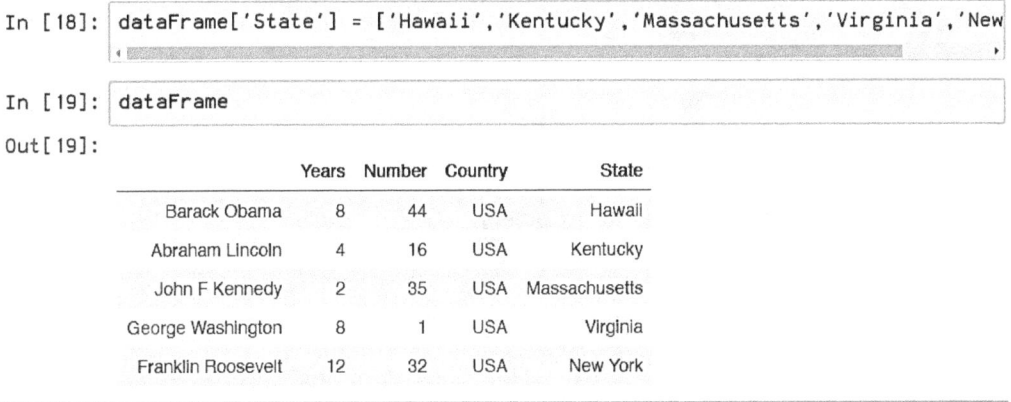

	Years	Number	Country	State
Barack Obama	8	44	USA	Hawaii
Abraham Lincoln	4	16	USA	Kentucky
John F Kennedy	2	35	USA	Massachusetts
George Washington	8	1	USA	Virginia
Franklin Roosevelt	12	32	USA	New York

We pass the columns we want to add as a list followed by their corresponding values in respective order. Ensure to match the length of the DataFrame while assigning lists or arrays to a column to prevent occasions of missing data.

It is also important to note that assigning values to columns that do not exist will automatically create the column and assign to it the specified value.

To delete a column within a Pandas DataFrame, we use the del keyword, which is similar to how we delete a python dictionary. To illustrate column deletion, let us add a column called California and fill it with Boolean values—true if a president is from California and False if not.

```
In [21]: dataFrame['california'] = dataFrame.State == 'California'
```

```
In [22]: dataFrame
```
Out[22]:

	Years	Number	Country	State	california
Barack Obama	8	44	USA	Hawaii	False
Abraham Lincoln	4	16	USA	Kentucky	False
John F Kennedy	2	35	USA	Massachusetts	False
George Washington	8	1	USA	Virginia	False
Franklin Roosevelt	12	32	USA	New York	False

Using the del keyword, we can remove this column, as shown below:

```
In [23]: del dataFrame['california']
```

```
In [24]: dataFrame
```
Out[24]:

	Years	Number	Country	State
Barack Obama	8	44	USA	Hawaii
Abraham Lincoln	4	16	USA	Kentucky
John F Kennedy	2	35	USA	Massachusetts
George Washington	8	1	USA	Virginia
Franklin Roosevelt	12	32	USA	New York

Now, if we look at the existing columns within the DataFrame, we get four main columns:

```
In [25]: dataFrame.columns
Out[25]: Index(['Years', 'Number', 'Country', 'State'], dtype='object')
```

Upon performing the del operation on the DataFrame, the returned column contains an actual view of the underlying data, which means that the operation occurs in-place, and any modifications were undertaken on a section of the Pandas series also broadcasts to the original DataFrame.

You can copy a part of the Pandas array using the copy method. If a DataFrame does not have index and column name set, you can use the name attribute to accomplish this as shown below:

```
In [37]: dataFrame.index.name = ''; dataFrame.columns.name='Name'

In [38]: dataFrame
Out[38]:
```

Name	Years	Number	Country	State
Barack Obama	8	44	USA	Hawaii
Abraham Lincoln	4	16	USA	Kentucky
John F Kennedy	2	35	USA	Massachusetts
George Washington	8	1	USA	Virginia
Franklin Roosevelt	12	32	USA	New York

To get the values contained in a DataFrame, you can use the values attribute, which returns a two-dimensional Numpy ndarrays, which is similar to the Pandas Series.

```
In [40]: dataFrame.values
Out[40]: array([[8, 44, 'USA', 'Hawaii'],
                [4, 16, 'USA', 'Kentucky'],
                [2, 35, 'USA', 'Massachusetts'],
                [8, 1, 'USA', 'Virginia'],
                [12, 32, 'USA', 'New York']], dtype=object)
```

In a scenario where the DataFrame's columns are of different data types, the data type of the values array is automatically set to accommodate all the columns in the DataFrame.

Now that one of the most common ways to create a Pandas has been talked about, let us look at some of the other types you can pass to the DataFrame function to create the DataFrame.

- A dictionary of dictionaries: Converts each inner dictionary to columns and merges the keys to form a row index.

- Two-dimensional Numpy array: Creates a DataFrame using the passed data. You can pass row and column labels but this optional.

```
In [51]: array = np.random.rand(5,5)

In [54]: new_dataFrame = pd.DataFrame(array)

In [55]: new_dataFrame
Out[55]:
```

	0	1	2	3	4
0	0.102508	0.985205	0.102353	0.851598	0.868762
1	0.070646	0.544700	0.461856	0.992644	0.549548
2	0.171221	0.953029	0.303306	0.606748	0.186475
3	0.661022	0.165850	0.575924	0.090192	0.708701
4	0.107004	0.267388	0.155782	0.381335	0.159968

- Numpy Masked Array

- Another Pandas DataFrame

- List of dictionaries

- List of series

- Numpy Structured array

Pandas Series

A Pandas series refers to a one-dimensional array-like object that contains a series of values—similar to a Numpy array and an associated array of labels called an index. We can create the simplest Pandas series using a Numpy array, as shown below:

```
In [2]: array = np.arange(0,20)

In [3]: series = pd.Series(array)

In [4]: series
Out[4]: 0     0
        1     1
        2     2
        3     3
        4     4
        5     5
```

The above prints a Pandas series with all values from the Numpy array—generated using the arange function—and the index. The output above shows the index of the Pandas series on the Left and the actual values on the right.

As we did not specify the index we want to be used, a default index made up of integers 0 through N − 1 - where N is the length of the data—is used. Using a Pandas series values and index attributes, we can also get the array representation and index object of the Pandas series.

```
In [8]: series.index
Out[8]: RangeIndex(start=0, stop=20, step=1)

In [7]: series.values # use value attribute
Out[7]: array([ 0,  1,  2,  3,  4,  5,  6,  7,  8,  9, 10, 11, 12, 13, 14, 15, 16,
               17, 18, 19])
```

The best way is to create a Pandas series with index identifying each data point with a specified data label as shown:

```
In [9]: indexed_Series = pd.Series([100,250,400,550,700], index=['OR','MI','MA','CA','VE'])

In [10]: indexed_Series
Out[10]: OR    100
         MI    250
         MA    400
         CA    550
         VE    700
         dtype: int64
```

For Pandas series, we can use the data labels in the index to select a single group of specific values.

```
In [12]: indexed_Series['CA']
Out[12]: 550
```

This case is also true while selecting multiple elements using their respective indices.

```
In [13]: indexed_Series[['CA','OR','MA']]
Out[13]: CA    550
         OR    100
         MA    400
         dtype: int64
```

In the code above, the arguments ['CA', 'OR,' 'MA] interpret as a list of indices, although it contains string type instead of integers.

It is also good to note that using Numpy operations or Numpy-like operations such as logical filtering, scalar multiplication, or mathematical functions call will not alter the index values:

```
In [15]: np.exp(indexed_Series)
Out[15]: OR     2.688117e+43
         MI     3.746455e+108
         MA     5.221470e+173
         CA     7.277212e+238
         VE     1.014232e+304
         dtype: float64
```

As you can see, doing this preserves the indices of the elements while it subjects the actual values to a mathematical exponential function.

You can also think of a Pandas series as a dictionary of fixed length where the indices represent the keys of dictionaries, and the actual values are the array elements. You can also pass a normal python dictionary to the Pandas Series function to create a series of elements.

```
In [22]: indexed_Series.index = ['A','B','C','D','E']

In [23]: indexed_Series
Out[23]: A    100
         B    250
         C    400
         D    550
         E    700
         dtype: int64

In [19]: my_dict = {"OR": 100, "MI": 250, "MA": 400, "CA": 550, "VE": 700}

In [20]: pd.Series(my_dict)
Out[20]: OR    100
         MI    250
         MA    400
         CA    550
         VE    700
         dtype: int64
```

A Pandas series assigns a value of NaN (Not a Number) to missing values. If a value is missing an index, the Pandas Series does not include it. We use the functions isnull and notnull to detect missing data.

Indexing, Selection, and Slicing

We can use the Pandas series indexing technique to select subsections of the Pandas DataFrame.

Example:

```
In [57]: dataFrame["Years"]
Out[57]:
         Barack Obama         8
         Abraham Lincoln      4
         John F Kennedy       2
         George Washington    8
         Franklin Roosevelt   12
         Name: Years, dtype: int64
```

NOTE: This only selects the integral section of the DataFrame.

Slicing a Pandas data structure, however, behaves differently from the usual python slicing technique as the end value is inclusive.

Plotting and Visualization

With some of that in mind, let us dive a bit more into what matplotlib is all about and how we can utilize this for some of our own needs as well. This is a plotting library that we will use for things like 2D graphs while working with machine learning and data analysis in the Python language. We can use it for many options like web application servers, python scripts, python scripts, and some of the other graphical interface toolkits.

Python Matplotlib Prerequisites

The distinct Info Visualization libraries offer a great scope of programming interfaces terrific for altogether one-of-a-kind kinds of consumers and more than a few techniques for making representations. These APIs contrast through requests of greatness in how lots code is expected to do primary errands and in how tons control they provide to the consumer to deal with out of the ordinary undertakings and for creating natives into new types of plots:

Article located Matplotlib API: Matplotlib's main API, permitting full control and compositionality then again thinking boggling and distinctly verbose for some primary undertakings like making subfigures.

Basic Pyplot API: Matplotlib's indispensable interface lets in Matlab-style primary directions, which are short for straightforward cases yet now not compositional and in this manner generally limited to a precise association of bolstered choices.

Basic Pandas .plot() APIs: Centered around dataframes, the place purchasers will essentially set up the facts in Pandas, at that point, pick out a subset for plotting. As will be talked about in the following post in this arrangement, in modern times upheld for an extensive scope of diagramming libraries and furthermore for other statistics structures, making them a valuable critical arrangement of appreciably bolstered quintessential plotting directions. Not straightforwardly compositional, but can return composable articles from a hidden plotting library (with appreciation to hvPlot).

- Revelatory illustrations APIs: The Grammar of Graphics-propelled libraries like ggplot, plotnine, Altair, and (somewhat) Bokeh give an attribute technique to shape graphical natives like tomahawks and glyphs to make a full plot.

- Definitive records APIs: Building on the local APIs for exceptional libraries, HoloViews and GeoViews give a lot greater degree of decisive and compositional API concentrating on explaining, depicting, and working with visualizable information, as opposed to plot components.

Every one of these APIs is healthy to purchasers with a variety of foundations and objectives, making a few undertakings easy and compact, and others more and more troublesome. Aside from Matplotlib, most libraries bolster one or at most two optional APIs, making it indispensable to pick a library whose method matches with every client's specialized foundation and appreciated work processes.

Types of Plots

You can actually work with quite a few different plots and graphs. We can pick out the one that is best for our needs, and it depends on the kind of data that you want to work with, and how you can visualize this information the best as well. We are going to look at a few of the codes that you can use to create these plots and see the best results possible.

First, let us start out with a very basic plot that we can do in this library to generate a simple graph. Open up your compiler in Python and type in the code below to see how this can work:

```
from matplotlib import pyplot as plt
```

#Plotting to our canvas

```
plt.plot([1,2,3],[4,5,1])
```

#Showing what we plotted

```
plt.show()
```

Therefore, with just a few lines of code, you will be able to generate a basic graph with this kind of library. It is just that simple to work with. We can then take this simple code and add in a few other parts. We can add titles, labels, and more to the graph that is seen in the library in order to bring in some more meaning to it.

Formatting Your Python Plot

It is also possible to go through with this and try out some of the different styling techniques so that the graph is going to look the way that you would like. You could go through and change up the color or the width of a particular line in the graph, or you could add in a few grid lines if you would like. Therefore, we need to be able to learn how to add in some of the stylings when it comes to these graphs with matplotlib. First, remember that we need to be able to import the style package from our matplotlib library, and then we need to use the styling function to do the rest.

Now that we have been able to create a pretty basic code for a basic graph, we can go through and be a bit more specific about what we are doing on all of this and make it a little easier to handle. We are going to make our own bar graph in this library so that we can compare the data we have and more. A bar graph is going to work with bars so that we can compare the data that is found through different categories. It is going to be suited well when we want to be able to see how changes are going to happen over a certain period, based on what we want. You can make this bar graph go either vertically or horizontally. With this one, when you have a bar that is longer than the others are, it means that the value is higher. With this in mind, the coding that we need to use to make our bar graph is below:

```
from matplotlib import pyplot as plt

plt.bar([0.25,1.25,2.25,3.25,4.25],[50,40,70,80,20],
label="BMW",width=.5)
plt.bar([.75,1.75,2.75,3.75,4.75],[80,20,20,50,60],
label="Audi", color='r',width=.5)
plt.legend()
plt.xlabel('Days')
plt.ylabel('Distance (kms)')
plt.title('Information')
plt.show()
```

We can also take some of the same ideas and use them to make our own histogram. There is a difference present between the bar graph that we did above and a histogram. The histogram is going to be used to show distribution, but then the bar chart is going to be used to help us compare a few different entities to one another. These are going to be the most useful when you have arrays or a list that is long.

We are going to look at an example of how to make some of these for our own needs. We are going to do an example where we are able to plot out the population's age based on which bin they fall into. This bin is going to be important because it will consist of a range in most cases. The bins often want to be similar in size to one another to make them as even as possible. We are going to use the code below, which will give us intervals often. This means we work from 0 to 9, 10 to 19, and so on.

Python Matplotlib Keyword Strings

We're giving an assessment of 10 interdisciplinary Python facts representation libraries, from the awesome to the dark.

Matplotlib

Matplotlib is the O.G. of Python information grasp libraries. Despite being over 10 years old, it's as but the most greatly utilized library for plotting in the Python human beings group. It was supposed to closely take after MATLAB, a restrictive programming language created during the 1980s.

Since matplotlib was the principal Python information representation library, numerous unique libraries are based totally on it or intended to work with it in the course of the investigation. A few libraries like pandas and Seaborn are "wrappers" over matplotlib. They enable you to get to some of matplotlib's techniques with much less code.

While matplotlib is useful for getting a feeling of the information, it is no longer particularly helpful for making distribution outlines swiftly and effectively. As Chris Moffitt calls interest to in his evaluation of Python representation devices, matplotlib "is fantastically ground-breaking then again with that electricity comes multifaceted nature."

Matplotlib has for pretty some time been condemned for its default styles, which have a precise Nineteen Nineties feel. The up and coming arrival of matplotlib 2.0 ensures several new style modifications to tackle this issue.

Seaborn

Seaborn outfits the intensity of matplotlib to make first-rate graphs in a couple of lines of code. The key difference is Seaborn's default patterns and shading palettes, which are meant to be all the greater tastefully pleasant and present day. Since Seaborn is primarily based on matplotlib, you will have to know matplotlib to trade Seaborn's defaults.

Ggplot

Ggplot relies upon on ggplot2, a R plotting framework, and ideas from The Grammar of Graphics. Ggplot works uniquely in distinction to matplotlib: it gives you a hazard to layer components to make a whole plot. For example, you can begin with tomahawks, at that point include focuses, at that point, a line, a trendline, and so forth. In spite of the fact that The Grammar of Graphics has been adulated as an "instinctive" approach for plotting, prepared matplotlib consumers may want time to acclimate to this new outlook.

As indicated by way of the maker, ggplot isn't supposed to make profoundly tweaked illustrations. It penances unpredictability for an extra straightforward method for plotting.

Ggplot is firmly coordinated with pandas, so it's ideal to shop your statistics in a DataFrame when making use of ggplot.

Bokeh

Like ggplot, Bokeh relies upon on The Grammar of Graphics, alternatively no longer at all like ggplot, it is neighbor to Python, no longer ported over from R. Its high-quality lies in the ability to make intuitive, web-prepared plots, which can be efficaciously yield as JSON objects, HTML records, or smart net applications. Bokeh likewise helps spilling and continuous information.

Bokeh furnishes three interfaces with transferring stages of control to oblige specific purchaser types. The most extended degree is for making outlines rapidly. It incorporates strategies for making regular graphs, for example, bar plots, field plots, and histograms. The middle level has a similar particularity as matplotlib and enables you to control the essential structure squares of each graph (the dabs in a disperse plot, for instance). The most decreased stage is designed for engineers and programming engineers. It has no pre-set defaults and expects you to characterize every element of the outline.

Pygal

Like Bokeh and Plotly, pygal presents intuitive plots that can be inserted in the web browser. Its high differentiator is the capacity to yield outlines as SVGs. For something size of time that you are working with littler datasets, SVGs will do you best and dandy. However, in case you are making outlines with a large wide variety of information focuses, they'll journey issue rendering and come to be languid.

Since every outline kind is bundled into a method and the inherent styles are beautiful, it's whatever but tough to make a quality looking diagram in a couple of lines of code.

Plotly

You might also recognize Plotly as an on-line stage for statistics perception, but did you likewise realize you can get to its abilities from a Python scratch pad? Like Bokeh, Plotly's strong point is making wise plots, but it gives a few outlines you may not discover in many libraries, comparable to shape plots, dendograms, and 3D graphs.

Geoplotlib

Geoplotlib is a tool package for making maps and plotting geological information. You can make use of it to make an assortment of information types, as choropleths, heatmaps, and speck thickness maps. You should have Pyglet (an article located programming interface) added to utilize geoplotlib. Regardless, because most Python data appreciation libraries don't provide maps, it's fantastic to have a library dedicated exclusively to them.

Glimmer

Glimmer is motivated by using R's Shiny bundle. It permits you to seriously change examinations into intuitive net applications utilizing simply Python contents, so you do not want to recognise some other dialects like HTML, CSS, or JavaScript. Glimmer works with any Python records representation library. When you've got made a plot, you can fabricate fields over it so clients can channel and kind information.

Data Aggregation and Grouping Operations

This represents the first part of aggregation and clustering using Pharo DataFrame. This will only handle the basic functionality like clustering a data series using values of a separate series of corresponding size and using aggregation functions to the grouped data structures.

The next iterations will deal with functionality extended based on the targeted scenarios. The implementation is likely to change into something optimized.

Definition of Data Frame

This represents spreadsheet such as data structures that deliver an API for cleaning, slicing, and analyzing data.

In case you want to read more about the DataFrame project, you need to consider the documentation.

Split-Apply-Combine

The split-apply-combine is a technique where you categorize a certain task into manageable parts and then integrate all the parts together.

The data aggregation and grouping facilitates the production of summaries for analysis and display. For example, when you calculate the average values or creating a table of counts. This is a step that adheres to the split-apply-combine procedure.

1. Separate the data into sections based on a given procedure.
2. Use the function to every cluster independently.
3. Combine the results using a data structure.

Implementation

In this part, you will discover how the grouping and aggregation function is being implemented. In case you don't want these details, you can skip to the next part.

```
firstSeries groupBy: secondSeries.
```

Take, for instance, this message that has been sent to firstSeries object:

Once this message is sent, firstSeries will define an object of DataSeriesGrouped, which divides firstSeries into various subseries depending on the values of secondSeries.

The collection of subseries is later kept as an object of DataSeries whose keys are equivalent to the special values of the secondSeries and values store the subseries of firstSeries. That will match each of those unique values.

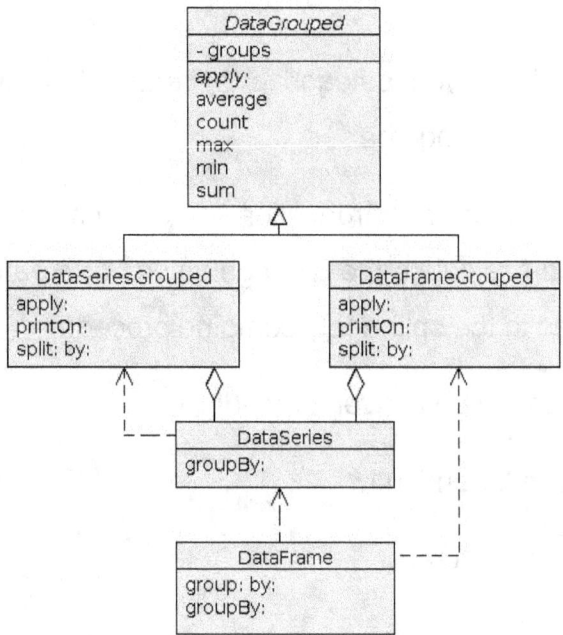

This means that the groups represent DataSeries that contain keys that match the unique values contained in a string in which the data frame is recognized. When the data frame is categorized by a single column, that column is removed from the data frame before grouping. Therefore, this eliminates data duplication because the same values will be preserved as keys.

In the case of DataSeriesGrouped, each subsystem will connect to a scalar, and all subsequent scalars will be merged into a DataSeries. When it comes to DataFrameGrouped, it will include the block in each column of each subdirectory box and display the final scalar table as the new DataFrame.

The combination is done with the use of messages. It requires a block as an argument and uses it on every value in the group string, and then integrates it into a new data structure.

The most common aggregation functions, such as average, minimum, and maximum, deliver smaller messages. In the next iteration, these messages are useful and act as shortcuts.

```
average
    ^ self apply: [ :each | each average ].
```

However, these messages will carry the optimized implementations of the likened aggregations because these functions must be time and memory efficient.

Let's examine the grouping series.

The easiest example of using this groupBy operator is to classify the values of a series using values of the same size.

```
bill := tips column: #total_bill.
sex  := tips column: #sex.bill groupBy: sex.
```

The result of the above query will be an object. This object will separate the bill into two series.

Because a lot of time, you need to classify the group series that resemble columns of a single data frame. There is a useful shortcut.

How to Group Data Frames?

Besides the shortcut for classifying columns. The DataFrame has a method for classifying one of its columns.

The response of the above query will be an object of DataFrameGrouped, keeping two different data frames for smokers and non-smokers.

The smoker column will be removed from the above data frames because its values will be kept as keys within a DataFrameGrouped object. Additionally, the different groups of smokers and non-smokers will enable the complete reconstruction of the smoker column when needed.

The aggregation functions represent the ones that accept different input and display a scalar value that sums up the values of that particular series. These refer to statistical functions such as min, max, stdev, and many more.

Once the data has been combined, next, you can use the aggregation function to get the integrated data structure that sums up the original data.

```
grouped := tips group: #total_bill by: #day.
grouped apply: [ :each | each average round: 2].
```

Since the grouping is being done to a column of DataFrame by a separate column, the result will be a DataSeries object.

As said before, the DataGrouped presents shortcuts for popularly applied aggregation functions such as count, sum, min, and max. At the moment, these are shortcuts, but in the future, they will execute the optimized aggregations that will be used faster.

Once the data box has been grouped into a DataFrameGrouped object, we can also apply an aggregate function to that object. DataFrameGrouped implements the apply message: for the function to apply to every column in every child data frame, producing the incremental value. These steps are then combined into a new data frame.

The result of this query will be a data box containing the number of empty cells for each column, corresponding to 'Male' and 'Female' rows

```
        | total_bill   tip  smoker   day  time  size
--------+-------------------------------------------
Female  | 87           87   87       87   87    87
Male    | 157          157  157      157  157   157
```

Introduction to Modeling Libraries in Python

We have talked about Data Analysis, and now it is time to take some of that information and put it to good use. You are probably interested in deep learning, and maybe even in making some of your Convolutional Neural Networks, but are wondering where you should start. The best step is to pick out the library that you want to use. But this brings up another challenge because there are just so many coding libraries out there that you can choose from, and all of them have some amazing power and features behind them.

To start with, we are going to take a look at some of the best Python libraries that can help with deep learning. Other languages can help with things like machine learning and deep learning. But for most of the tasks that you want to do, especially if you are a beginner in Data Analysis and all of the processes that we have been talking about, then Python is going to be the choice for you. Even within Python, there are several libraries that you can choose from to get your deep learning work done. So, with that in mind, let's dive right in and see some of the best Python deep learning libraries that you can use for your Data Analysis.

Caffe

It is pretty hard to get started with a look at deep learning libraries through Python without spending some time talking about the Caffe library. It is likely that if you have done any research on deep learning at all, then you have heard about Caffe and what it can do for some of the projects and models that you want to create.

While Caffe is technically not going to be a Python library, it is going to provide us with some bindings into the Python language. We are going to use these bindings when it is time to deploy the network in the wild, rather than just when we try to train the model. The reason that we are going to include it in this Phase is that it is used pretty much everywhere and on all of the parts of a deep learning model that you need to create.

Theano

The next kind of library that we can work with is known as Theano. This one has helped to develop and work with a lot of the other deep learning libraries that we have that work with Python. In the same way that a programmer would not be able to have some options like scikit-image, scikit-learn, and SciPy without NumPy, the same thing can be said when we talk about Theano and some of the other higher-level abstractions and libraries that come with deep learning.

When we take a look at the core of this, Theano is going to be one of the Python libraries that not only helps out with deep learning, but can be used to define, optimize, and evaluate a lot of mathematical expressions that will involve multi-dimensional arrays. Theano is going to accomplish this because it is tightly integrated with the NumPy library, and it keeps its use of GPU pretty transparent overall. While you can use the Theano library to help build up some deep learning networks, this one is often seen as the building blocks of these neural networks, just like how the NumPy library is going to serve as the building blocks when we work on scientific computing. Most of the other libraries that we will talk about as we progress through all of this are going to wrap around the Theano library, which makes it more accessible and convenient than some of the other options.

TensorFlow

Similar to what we can find with the Theano library, TensorFlow is going to be an option that is open-sourced and can work with numerical computation with the help of a data flow graph. This one was originally developed to be used with research on the Google Brain Team within Google's Machine Intelligence organization. And this library, since that time, has turned into an open-sourced option so that the general public can use it for their deep learning and data science needs.

One of the biggest benefits that we are going to see with the TensorFlow library, compared to what we see with Theano, is that it is able to work with distributed computing. This is particularly true when we look at multiple-GPUs for our project, though Theano is working on improving this one as well.

Keras

Many programmers find that they love working with the Keras library when it comes to performing models and other tasks with deep learning. Keras is seen as a modular neural network library that is more minimalistic than some of the others that we talk about. This one can use either TensorFlow or Theano as the backend so you can choose the one that works the best for any needs you have. The primary goal that comes with this library is that you should be able to experiment on your models quickly and get from the idea that you have over to the result as fast as possible.

Many programmers like this library because the networks that you architect are going to feel almost natural and easy, even as a beginner. It is going to include some of the best algorithms out there for optimizers, normalization, and even activation layers, so this is a great one to use if your process includes these.

If you want to get your network trained as fast as possible, working with a library like MXNet may be a better choice. But if you are looking to tune your hyperparameters, then you may want to work with the capability of Keras to set up four independent experiments and then evaluate how the results are similar or different between each of these.

Sklearn-Theano

There are going to be times when working with deep learning when you will want to train a CNN end-to-end. And then there are times when this is not needed. Instead, when this is not needed, you can treat your CNN as the feature extractor. This is going to be the most useful with some situations you may encounter where there is just not enough data to train the CNN from scratch. So, with this one, just pass your input images through a popular pre-trained architecture that can include some options like VGGNet, AlexNet, and OverFeat. You can then use these pre-trained options and extract features from the layer that you want, usually the FC layers.

Nolearn

A good library for you to work with is the Nolearn library. This is a good one to help out with some initial GPU experiments, especially with a MacBook Pro. It is also a good library to help out with performing some deep learning on an Amazon EC2 GPU instance.

While Keras wraps TensorFlow and Theano into a more user-friendly API, you will find that the Nolearn library will be able to do the same, but it will do this with the Lasagna library. Also, all of the code that we find with Nolearn is going to be compatible with Scikit-Learn, which is a big bonus for a lot of the projects that you want to work with.

Digits

The first thing to notice with this library is that it isn't considered a true deep learning library. Although it is written out in Python and it stands for Deep Learning GPU Training System. The reason for this is because this library is more of a web application that can be used for training some of the models of deep learning that you create with the help of Caffe. You could work with the source code a bit to work with a backend other than Caffe, but this is a lot of extra work in the process. And since the Caffe library is pretty good at what it does, and can help with a lot of the deep learning tasks that you want to accomplish, it is not worth your time.

If you have ever spent some time working with the Caffe library in the past, you can already attest to the fact that it is tedious to define your .prototxt files, generate the set of data for the image, run the network, and babysit the network training with the terminal that you are provided. The good news here is that the DIGITS library aims to fix all of this by allowing you to complete a lot of these tasks, if not all of these tasks, just from your browser. So, it may not be a deep learning library per se, but it does come into use when you struggle with the Caffe library.

In addition to all of the benefits above, the interface that the user gets to interact with is seen as excellent. This is because it can provide us with some valuable statistics and graphs to help you rain your model more effectively. You can also easily visualize some of the activation layers of the network to help with various inputs as needed. And finally, another benefit that is possible with this library is that if you come in with a specific image that you want to test, you have a few options on how to get this done. The first choice is to upload the image over to the DIGITS server. Alternatively, you can enter the URL that comes with the image, and then the model you make with Caffe will automatically be able to classify the image and display the results that you want in the browser.

Python is one of the best coding languages available for helping with tasks like deep learning, machine learning, and even with the topic of artificial intelligence, which encompasses both of the other two ideas. Other languages can handle the deep learning that we have been talking about, but none are going to be as effective, as powerful, have as many options, or be designed for a beginner in the way that Python can.

This is why we have focused our attention on the Python language and some of the best libraries that we can choose to help with a variety of deep learning tasks. Each of these libraries can come on board with your project and will provide a unique set of functions and skills to get the job done. Take a look through some of these libraries and see which one is going to be just right for your Data Analysis and for providing you with great insights while completing deep learning.

Conclusion

This is the end of the Python for Data Analysis book. The next milestone is to make the best use of your new-found wisdom of Python programming, data science, data analysis, and machine learning that have resulted in the birth of the powerhouse, which is the "Silicon Valley." So many companies, that span a lot of different industries, can benefit when they work with data analysis. This allows them to get a lot of the power and control that they want for their respective industries and will ensure that they will be able to really impress their customers and get some good results in the process. Learning how to use a data analysis is going to change the game in how you do business, as long as it is used properly.

This guidebook has been organized well to explore what data analysis is all about, and how we can use this for our benefits as well. There are a lot of business tools out there, but data analysis is designed to help us focus on finding the hidden patterns and insights that are in our data, making it easier to base our decisions on data, rather than intuition and guessing as we did in the past. And when it comes to making sure that we complete the data analysis in the right manner, nothing is better than working with the Python coding language to get things done.

There are so many aspects that need to come into play when we are working with our own data analysis, and we must take the time to learn how these works, and how to put it all together. And that is exactly what we will do in this guidebook. When you are ready to learn more about Python data analysis, and all of the different parts that come together to help us with understanding our data and how to run our business, make sure to recheck this guide to help you.

You would also develop skills in loading and exporting dataset from and to Python environments.

There is so much more to Data Analysis than the corporate and government decisions. As a programmer, you are venturing into an industry that is challenging and exciting at the same time.

Generally, this book has provided you with a guide on to use these handy libraries in data analysis. Once you have acquired these skills and know the functionalities of the NumPy, Pandas, and Matplotlib libraries, you will be able to analyze any data you have in hand using Python. You also develop more advanced skills to handle complex datasets.

Now that you have finished reading this book and mastered the use of Python programming, you are all set to start developing your own Python-based machine learning model as well as performing big data analysis using all the open sources readily available and explicitly described in this book. You can position yourself to use your deep knowledge and understanding of all the cutting edge technologies obtained from this book to contribute to the growth of any company and land yourself a new high paying and rewarding job!

CHAPTER - 3

Python For Data Science

Dylan Penny

Introduction

When handling data, the most common, traditional, and widely used management technique is the 'Relational Database Management Systems,' also known as 'RDBMS.' This technique is applied to almost every dataset, as it easily meets the dataset's required demands of the processing; however, this is not the case for 'Big Data.' Before we can understand why such management techniques fail to process big data, we need to understand first what the term 'Big Data' refers to. The name itself gives away a lot of the information regarding the data natures. Nevertheless, big data is basically a term that is used to define a collection of datasets that are very large and complex in size alone. Such datasets become difficult to process using traditional data management techniques and, thus, demand a new approach for handling them, as it is evident from the fact that the commonly used technique RDBMS has zero working compatibility with big data.

The core of data science is to employ methods and techniques that are the most suitable for the analysis of the sample dataset so we can take out the essential bits of information contained in it. In other words, big data is like a raw mineral ore containing a variety of useful materials, but in its current form, its contents are unusable and useless. Data science is the refinery, which essentially uses effective techniques to analyze this ore and then employ corresponding methods to extract its contents for us to use.

The world of big data is exponentially vast and the use of data science with big data can be seen in almost every sector of the modern age, be it commercial, non-commercial, business, or even industrial settings. For instance, in a commercial setting, the corresponding companies use the data science and big data elements to chiefly get a better insight into the demands of their customers and information regarding the efficiency of their products, staff, manufacturing processes, etc. Consider Google's advertising department AdSense; it basically employs data science to analyze the big data (which is a collection of user internet data) to extract information in order to ensure that the person browsing the internet is seeing relevant advertisements. The uses of data science extend far and beyond what we can imagine. It is not possible to list all the advantageous uses that are currently being employed in the modern-day. However, what we do know is that the majority of the datasets gathered by big companies all around the world are none other than big data. Data science is essential for these companies to analyze this data and benefit from the information it contains. Not only that, big educational institutions like Universities and research work also benefit from data science.

While venturing across the field of data science, you will soon come to realize that there is not one defined type of data. Instead, there are multiple categories under which data is classified, and each category of data requires an entirely different toolset in order to be processed.

Following are the seven major categories of data:

1. Structured Data.
2. Unstructured Data.
3. Natural Language Data.
4. Machine Generated Data.
5. Graph-based Data.
6. Audio, Video, and Image Data.
7. Streaming Data.

As the name suggests, a collection of data that is organized according to a defined model and restricted in the record's corresponding data fields is known as structured data. For instance, data that is organized in the form of a table is known as structured data (such as Excel tables or in databases). To manage and analyze such data, a preferable method is to use the Structured Query Language or SQL. However, not all structured datasets are easily manageable; for instance, the family data tree is also a structured dataset, but it becomes difficult to process and analyze such structured datasets. In other words, some exceptions in these data categories may demand another data processing technique.

Raw data is never structured; it is brought into a defined setting by the users. Hence, if we are given a data sample that is structured, then all is good; however, if the data is unstructured, we must bring it into a structured format before applying the SQL technique.

Below is an example showing a dataset structured into an Excel table:

	Indicator ID	Dimension List	Timeframe	Numeric Value	Missing Value Flag	Confidence Int
1						
2	214390830	Total (Age-adjusted)	2008	74.6%		73.8%
3	214390833	Aged 18-44 years	2008	59.4%		58.0%
4	214390831	Aged 18-24 years	2008	37.4%		34.6%
5	214390832	Aged 25-44 years	2008	66.9%		65.5%
6	214390836	Aged 45-64 years	2008	88.6%		87.7%
7	214390834	Aged 45-54 years	2008	86.3%		85.1%
8	214390835	Aged 55-64 years	2008	91.5%		90.4%
9	214390840	Aged 65 years and over	2008	94.6%		93.8%
10	214390837	Aged 65-74 years	2008	93.6%		92.4%
11	214390838	Aged 75-84 years	2008	95.6%		94.4%
12	214390839	Aged 85 years and over	2008	96.0%		94.0%
13	214390841	Male (Age-adjusted)	2008	72.2%		71.1%
14	214390842	Female (Age-adjusted)	2008	76.8%		75.9%
15	214390843	White only (Age-adjusted)	2008	73.8%		72.9%
16	214390844	Black or African American only (Age-adjusted)	2008	77.0%		75.0%
17	214390845	American Indian or Alaska Native only (Age-adjusted)	2008	66.5%		57.1%
18	214390846	Asian only (Age-adjusted)	2008	80.5%		77.7%
19	214390847	Native Hawaiian or Other Pacific Islander only (Age-adjusted)	2008	DSU		
20	214390848	2 or more races (Age-adjusted)	2008	75.6%		69.6%

Data found in emails, is a common example of unstructured data. Hence to process and analyze the data, we must first filter it and bring it into a structured form.

One may argue that data contained in an email is also structured to some extent because there are fields such as the sender, the receiver, and the subject. However, the reason why traditional structural data analyzing techniques are not applicable to emails is that the data contained within them are either highly varying or context-specific. Moreover, the choice of words, the language used, and the intonations to refer to something in an email also varies, making the task even more complicated.

This is also a type of unstructured data, and it is also very complicated to process as we would need to factor in linguistics. Hence, for such datasets, the user must have a good understanding of various data science techniques in addition to linguistics. The main concern of the community working with natural language processing is the lack of generalization in their models. Each model is trained specifically to one aspect, such as entity recognition, topic recognition, and summarization, etc., but these models fail to generalize over to other domains such as text completion and sentiment analysis. The reason is that language is ambiguous, and it is impossible to program and train machines to overcome this ambiguity when humans themselves have failed to do so.

As the name suggests, the data produced by a computer or its corresponding processes and applications without any external fiddling of humans is known as machine-generated data.

Such types of data have become a major data resource as it is automated. To analyze and extract the information being contained within this machine-generated data, we would need to use tools that are very scalable. This is in accordance with the fact that this type of data is not only high in volume but also in the speed to which it is being generated. Data such as crash logs, web server logs, network logs, and even call record logs are all in nature, machine-generated data as shown in the example below:

```
CSIPERF:TXCOMMIT;313236
2014-11-29 11:36:13, Info        CSI    00000153 Creating NT transaction (seq
69), objectname [6]"(null)"
2014-11-29 11:36:13, Info        CSI    00000154 Created NT transaction (seq 69)
result 0x00000000, handle @0x4e54
2014-11-29 11:36:13, Info        CSI    00000155@2014/11/29:10:36:13.471
Beginning NT transaction commit...
2014-11-29 11:36:13, Info        CSI    00000156@2014/11/29:10:36:13.705 CSI perf
trace:
CSIPERF:TXCOMMIT;273993
2014-11-29 11:36:13, Info        CSI    00000157 Creating NT transaction (seq
70), objectname [6]"(null)"
2014-11-29 11:36:13, Info        CSI    00000158 Created NT transaction (seq 70)
result 0x00000000, handle @0x4e5c
2014-11-29 11:36:13, Info        CSI    00000159@2014/11/29:10:36:13.764
Beginning NT transaction commit...
2014-11-29 11:36:14, Info        CSI    0000015a@2014/11/29:10:36:14.094 CSI perf
trace:
CSIPERF:TXCOMMIT;386259
2014-11-29 11:36:14, Info        CSI    0000015b Creating NT transaction (seq
71), objectname [6]"(null)"
2014-11-29 11:36:14, Info        CSI    0000015c Created NT transaction (seq 71)
result 0x00000000, handle @0x4e5c
2014-11-29 11:36:14, Info        CSI    0000015d@2014/11/29:10:36:14.106
Beginning NT transaction commit...
2014-11-29 11:36:14, Info        CSI    0000015e@2014/11/29:10:36:14.429 CSI perf
trace:
CSIPERF:TXCOMMIT;375591
```

We must not confuse the terms 'graph' and 'graph theory.' The first one represents the geometrical representation of data in a graph, and any data can be made into a graph, but that does not necessarily change the nature of the data. The latter refers to the mathematical structure, which essentially is a model that connects the objects into a pair based on their inherent relationship with each other. Hence, we can also term such categories of data as Network data. This type of data emphasizes elements such as the adjacency and relationship of objects and the common structures found in graphs found in graph-based data are:

- Nodes.
- Edges.
- Properties.

Graph-based data is most commonly seen on social media websites. Here's an example of a graph-based data representing many friends on a social network.

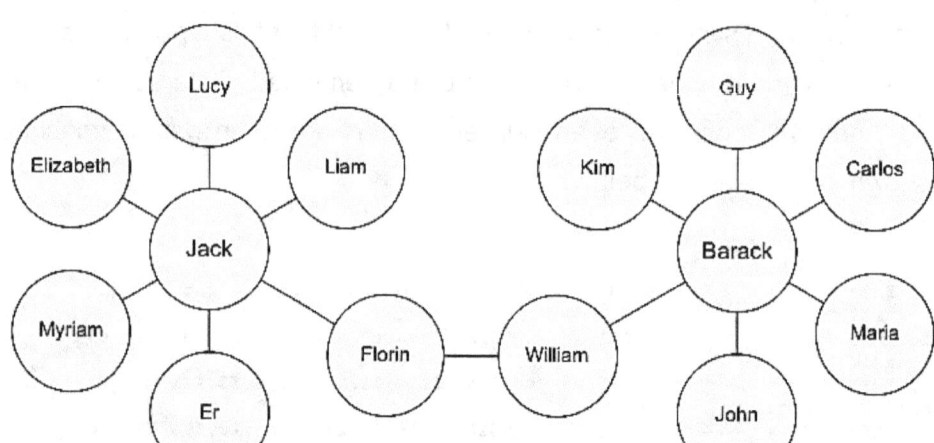

To query graph-based data, we normally use specialized query languages such as SPARQL.

Everyone is familiar with audio, image, and video data to a certain extent. However, out of all the data categories, audio, image, and video data are very difficult to deal with for a data scientist. This is partly because though we analyze this data, the computer must recognize elements, such as image data, discerning between objects, and identifying them is a very difficult task, although it is easy for the user. To deal with such categories of data, we usually implement deep learning models.

This category of data can take on the nature of any of the data categories mentioned previously. However, the aspect that makes it different from the other data categories is that in streaming data, the data only comes into the system after an event happens in real-time, unlike other categories where the data is loaded into the systems in the form of batches. The reason why streaming data is defined as an entirely different category is due to the fact that we need an altogether different process to analyze and extract information from streaming data.

Basic Python for Data Science

What Is Data Science?

Data science is a gathering of different instruments, data interfaces, and calculations with AI standards (algorithms) to find concealed patterns from raw data. This data is put away in big business data distribution warehouses and utilized in inventive approaches to create business value.

A data examiner (analyst) and a data scientist are unique. An analyst attempts to process the data history and clarify what is happening. Whereas a data researcher needs different propelled calculations of AI (algorithms of machine learning) for an event of a specific occasion by utilizing analysis.

Python and Its History

Python is a globally useful, high-quality, translated programming language. Developed by Guido van Rossum and first released in 1991, the Python Foundation emphasizes code clarity by making the most of critical space. Its language is developed and designed with object methodology to allow software engineers to compose clear and logical code for small and large-scale projects.

Python was first developed in the late 1980s as the successor to the ABC language. Python 2.0, released in 2000, featured snapshots, such as degradation concepts and a garbage collection framework, suitable for collecting reference cycles. Python 3.0, downloaded in 2008, was a notable language modification, and much of Python 2's code does not run unmodified in Python 3. Language designer Guido van Rossum was solely tasked with committing until July 2018, but he now shares management as one person on a five-member board.

Unique Features and Philosophy

Python is a versatile programming language that supports Object-Oriented Programming (OOP) and other practical computer program languages. Initially, it was not designed for data science, but as a field, professionals started using it for data analysis and it became a priority for data science. Many different standards are bolstered utilizing expansions, including a plan by contract and rationale programming. Likewise, it includes dynamic name goals (late authoritative), which tie technique and variable names during system operations. The standard library has two modules that actualize useful devices acquired from Haskell and Standard ML.

Unlike incorporating most of its utility into its core, Python was meant to be deeply scalable.

Python is moving toward less complex and less mixed scoring and structure, while allowing engineers to make decisions on their approach to coding. Contrary to the saying, "Perl there is more than one approach," Python understands that "there must be one, and ideally one, clear approach to doing this." Alex Martelli of the Python Software Foundation and author of the book Python says that "portraying something as 'sharp' is not a compliment to Python culture."

Python engineers have tried to keep a strategic distance from initial progress and lock in patches in unnecessary parts of CPython that will offer minimal speed increases at the expense of clarity. When speed is important, a Python software engineer can transfer basic sync capabilities to extensions written in dialects. For example, C or use PyPy, one in the time compiler name. Cython is also accessible, which interprets Python content in C and makes direct C-level API calls to the Python translator.

Python's progress has been vastly improved with the Python Enhancement Proposal (PEP) process. This included collecting community feedback on issues and recording decisions about the Python framework. The Python coding style is included in PEP 8. Excellent PEPs are rated and evaluated by the Python community and the Python dashboard.

Language improvement is compared to progress in using CPython reports. The mailing list, Python-dev, is the essential discussion on the evolution of the language. Specific issues are discussed in the Roundup debugger maintained at Python.org. Development was initially carried out on a self-supplied Mercurial source code repository until Python was moved to GitHub in January 2017.

CPython open discards are available in three types, which determine how much of the customization number is incremented.

Backward variations are where the code is required to break and should transfer naturally. The initial part of the configuration number increases. These vaccines are rare; for example, Custom 3.0 was downloaded eight years after 2.0.

Large or "standard" shots look like a clock and include new features. The second part of the form number increases. All major variants support bug fixes long after they are released.

Non-new error correction rejections occur at regular intervals and when a sufficient number of upstream errors have been corrected since the last discharge. Security vulnerabilities are also defined in these discards; the third and the last part of the form number increases.

Many alpha and beta downloads are also downloaded as a peek and for testing before final downloads. Although there is an unpleasant schedule for each exemption, it is often postponed if the password is not ready. The Python progress team checks the status of the code by running a huge set of unit tests during the upgrade and using the uninterruptible BuildBot join system. The Python engineering community has also contributed more than 86,000 programming modules. The real school conference for Python is PyCon. There are also excellent Python training programs, for example, Pyladies.

Python Applications

Python is known for its broadly useful nature that makes it relevant in practically every space of programming advancement. Python can be used in a plethora of ways for improvement; there are specifying application territories where Python can be applied.

- **Web-applications:** We can utilize Python to create web applications. It gives libraries to deal with web conventions; for example, HTML and XML, JSON, email handling, demand, beautiful soup, Feedparser, and so on. Additionally, there are Frameworks; for example, Django, Pyramid, Flask, and so on to structure and develop electronic applications. Some significant improvements are PythonWikiEngines, PythonBlogSoftware, and so on.

- **Desktop GUI applications:** Python gives a Tk-GUI library to create UI in a Python-based application. Another valuable toolbox includes wxWidgets, Kivy, and is useable on a few stages. The Kivy is well known for comp sing multitouch applications.

- **Software development:** Python is useful for programming-advanced processes. It functions as a help language and can be utilized for fabricating control and the board, testing, and so forth.

- **Scientific and numeric:** Python is mainstream and generally utilized in logical and numeric figuring. Some helpful libraries and bundles are SciPy, Pandas, IPython, and so forth. SciPy is a library used for the collection of bundles of designing, science, and arithmetic.

- **Business applications:** Python is utilized to manufacture business applications, like ERP and online business frameworks. Tryton is an abnormal state application stage.

- **Console based application:** It can be utilized for support-based applications. For instance: IPython.

- **Audio or video-based applications:** Python is great for playing out various assignments and can be utilized to create media applications. Some of the authentic applications are cplay, TimPlayer, and so on.

- **Enterprise applications:** Python can be utilized to make applications that can be utilized inside an Enterprise or an Organization. Some ongoing applications are Tryton, OpenERP, Picalo, etc.

- **Applications for images:** Utilizing Python, a few applications can be created for a picture. Various applications include VPython, Gogh, and imgSeek.

Why Python to Conduct Data Analysis

Different programming languages can be utilized for data science (for example SQL, Java, Matlab, SAS, R, and some more), yet Python is the most favored by data researchers among the various programming languages in this rundown. Python has some exceptional features, including:

- Python is solid and basic with the goal that it is anything but difficult to gain proficiency in the language. You don't have to stress over its linguistic structure on the off chance that you are an amateur. Its syntax is similar to English writing; that's why it is an easy to use programming language.

- Python supports almost all platforms, like Windows, Mac, and Linux.

- It has multiple data structures with which complex calculations can easily be simplified.

- Python is an open-source programming language that enables the data scientists to get pre-defined libraries and codes to perform their tasks.

- Python can perform data visualization, data investigation, and data control.
- Python serves different ground-breaking libraries for algorithms and logical calculations. Different complex logical figuring and AI calculations can be performed utilizing this language effectively in a moderately basic sentence structure.

Fundamentals of Machine Learning

As you start to spend some more time on machine learning and all that it has to offer, you will start to find that there are a lot of different learning algorithms that you can work with. As you learn more about these, you will be amazed at what they are able to do.

But before we give these learning algorithms the true time and attention that they need, we first need to take a look at some of the building blocks that make machine learning work the way that it should. This chapter is really going to give us some insight into how these building blocks work and will ensure that you are prepared to really get the most out of your learning algorithms in machine learning.

The Learning Framework

Now that we have gotten to this point in the process, it is time to take a closer look at some of the framework that is going to be present when you are working with machine learning. This is going to be based a bit on statistics, as well as the model that you plan to use when you work with machine learning (more on that in a moment). Let's dive into some of the different parts of the learning framework that you need to know in order to really get the most out of your machine learning process.

Let's say that you decide that it is time to go on vacation to a new island. The natives that you meet on this island are really interested in eating papaya, but you have very limited experience with this kind of food, but you decide that it is good to give it a try and head on down to the marketplace, hoping to figure out which papaya is the best and will taste good to you.

Now, you have a few options as to how you would figure out which papaya is the best for you. You could start by asking some people at the marketplace which papayas are the best. But since everyone is going to have their own opinion about it, you are going to end up with lots of answers. You can also use some of your past experiences to do it.

At some point or another, you have worked with fresh fruit. You could use this to help you to make a good choice. You may look at the color of the papaya and the softness to help you make a decision. As you look through the papaya, you will notice that there are a ton of colors, from dark browns to reds, and even different degrees of softness, so it is confusing to know what will work the best.

After you look at the papayas a little bit, you will want to come up with a model that you can use to help you to learn the best papaya for next time. We are going to call this model a formal statistical learning framework and there are going to be four main components to this framework that includes:

- Learner's input.
- Learner's output.
- A measure of success.
- Simple data generalization.

The first thing that we need to explore when it comes to the learning framework in machine learning is the idea of learner's input. To help us with this, we need to find a domain set and then put all of our focus on it. This domain can easily be an arbitrary set that you find within your chosen objects, and these are going to be known as the points that you will need to go through and label.

Once you have been able to go through and determine the best domain points and then their sets that you are most likely to use, then you will need to go through and create a label for the set that you are going to really want to use, and the ones that you would like to avoid. This helps you to make some predictions and test out how well you were at making the prediction.

Then you need to take a look back at the learner's output. Once you know what the inputs of the scenario are all going to be about, it is going to be time to work on a good output. The output is going to be the creation of a rule of prediction. This is sometimes going to show up by another name such as the hypothesis, classifier, and predictor, no matter what it is called, to take all of your points and give them a label.

In the beginning, with any kind of program that you do, you are going to make guesses because you aren't sure what is going to work the best. You, or the program, will be able to go through and use past experience to help you make some predictions. But often, it is going to be a lot of trial and error to see what is going to work the best.

Next, it is time to move on to the data generalization model. When you have been able to add in the input and the output with the learner, it is time to take a look at the part that is the data generalization model. This is a good model to work with because it ensures that you are able to base it on the probability distribution of the domain sets that you want to use.

It is possible that you will start out with all of this process and you will find that it is hard to know what the distribution is all about. This model is going to be designed to help you out, even if you don't know which ones to pick out from the beginning. You will, as you go through this, find out more about the distribution, which will help you to make better predictions along the way.

PAC Learning Strategies

While we have already talked about how you are able to set up some of your own hypothesis and good training data to work with the other parts we have discussed in the previous section, it is now time to move on to the idea of PAC learning and what this is going to mean when we are talking about machine learning. There are going to be two main confines and parameters that need to be found with this learning model including the output classifier and the accuracy parameter.

To start us off on this, we are going to take a look at what is known as the accuracy parameter. This is an important type of parameter because it is going to help us determine how often we will see correct predictions with the output classifier. These predictions have to be set up in a way that is going to be accurate but also is based on any information that you feed the program.

It is also possible for you to work with what is called the confidence parameter. This is a parameter that will measure out how likely it is that the predictor will end up being a certain level of accuracy. Accuracy is always important, but there are going to be times when the project will demand more accuracy than others. You want to check out the accuracy and learn what you are able to do to increase the amount of accuracy that you have.

Now, we need to look at some of the PAC learning strategies. There are a few ways that you will find useful when you are working on your projects. You will find that it is useful when you bring up some training data to check the accuracy of the model that you are using. If you think that a project you are working with is going to have some uncertainties, you would bring these into play to see how well that program will be able to handle any of these. Of course, with this kind of learning model, there are going to be some random training sets that show up, so watch out for those.

The Generalization Models

The next thing that we need to look at in learning the machine is the idea of generalization models. This means that when we look at generalization; we will see two components present and we want to be able to use both of these components in order to go through all of the data. The components that you should be present include the true error rate and the reliability assumption.

Any time that you want to work with the generalization model, and you are also able to meet with that reliability assumption; you can expect that the learning algorithm will provide you with really reliable results compared to the other methods, and then you will have a good idea of the distribution. Of course, even when you are doing this, the assumption is not always going to be the most practical thing to work with. If you see that the assumption doesn't look very practical, it means that you either picked out unrealistic standards or the learning algorithm that you picked was not the right way.

There are a lot of different learning algorithms that you are able to work with when you get into machine learning. Just because you choose one specific one, even if it is the one that the others want to work with, using one doesn't always give you a guarantee that you will get the hypothesis that you like at all. Unlike with the Bayes predictor, not all of these algorithms will be able to help you figure out the error rate type that is going to work for your business or your needs either.

In machine learning, you will need to make a few assumptions on occasion, and this is where some of the past experiences that you have are going to need to come into play to help you out. In some cases, you may even need to do some experimenting to figure out what you want to do. But machine learning can often make things a lot easier in the process.

These are some of the building blocks that you need to learn about and get familiar with when it comes to machine learning and all of the different things that you can do with this. You will find that it is possible to use all of these building blocks as we get into some of the learning algorithms that come with machine learning as we go through this guidebook.

Statistics and Probabilities

As you start to work with the process of machine learning, it is essential to know that there is going to be a friendly relationship that ends up showing between this process and what is called the probability theory. Machine learning is a pretty broad field to work with, and this means that it doesn't work on its own, but also with some other fields at the same time. The fields you will be able to work with often depend on the kind of project.

One thing that you are going to notice when you start with machine learning is that it can merge with statistics and probability. It is so crucial for a lot of the projects that you choose to start learning how these three different areas are going to work together.

Now, there are a few different methods that you can utilize with probability and statistics, and all of them are important to the learning process that you need to see happen here. The first thing to consider is picking out the right algorithm. And as you go through this guidebook, you will find that there are a lot of different algorithms that you can use, including supervised, unsupervised, and also reinforced learning algorithms. However, not all of the algorithms are going to work with every project that you have.

When you pick out one of the algorithms to work with (and we will talk about quite a few of these in this guidebook), there are a few things you need to balance out together, including the number of parameters that you need, the complexity, the training time that you can work with, and the accuracy. As we spend more time with machine learning, you will find that each project you need to focus on will ask for a specific combination of these factors, so consider that ahead of time.

When you decide to work with the ideas of statistics and the probability theory, you will be better prepared to pick out the right parameters for your specific program, the strategies for validation, and you can use all of these to pick out the algorithm for this project. This is also going to be helpful to use when you want to figure out the amount of uncertainty that is present in that algorithm, and you can determine if there is a level of trust that you should have for any predictions.

As you can imagine here, both of these two topics are going to be very useful when working on any project with machine learning, and they will do wonders when you want to understand what is going on with any project. This phase will look at the different topics that come with both statistics and the probability theory and how you can use them on any project.

What Are the Random Variables?

Now, the first topic in statistics is random variables. With probability theory, these random variables are going to be expressed with the "X" symbol, and it is the variable that has all its possible variables come out as numerical outcomes that will come up during one of your random experiments. With random variables, there are going to be either continuous or discrete options. This means that sometimes your random variables will be functions that will map outcomes to the real value inside their space. We will look at a few examples of this one to help it make sense later on.

We are going to start with an example of a random variable by throwing a die. The random variable that we are going to look at is going to be represented by X, and it will rely on the outcome that you will get once the die is thrown. The choices of X that would come naturally here is going to go through to map out the outcome denoted as 1 to the value of i.

What this means is that if X equals 1, you will map the event of throwing a one on your die to being the value of i. You would be able to map this out with any number that is on the die, and it is even possible to take it to the next step and pick out some mappings that are a bit strange. For example, you could map out Y to make it the outcome of 0. This can be a hard process to do, and we aren't going to spend much time on it, but it can help you to see how it works. When we are ready to write out this one, we would have the probability, which is shown as P of outcome 1 of random variable X. it would look like the following: $P_X(i)$ or $(x=i)$

Distribution

Now that we have looked a bit at the random variables, it is time to look a bit at the idea of a probability distribution, and how it works with machine learning. What is meant here is that we need to take a look at the outcomes and figure out the probability that they are going to happen, or a random variable to happen. To make this even easier, we are going to use this distribution to figure out how likely it is that we are going to get a specific number.

Let's say that you are working with a die. There are six sides to it, and you have a random probability of one of the numbers showing up each time you throw it. We can use the distribution to figure out how likely it is with a particular throw; we will get a five or a two or one of the other numbers.

To help us get started with this one, it helps to have an example. We will need to let the X, which is our random variable, but the outcome that we will see on the die when we throw it. We are also going to start this experiment using the assumption that the die is perfectly capable of being used with no tricks and it isn't loaded. This ensures that the sides all end up with the same probability of showing up each time you do a throw. The probability distribution you will work with here to figure out how probable it is that one number will show up includes

PX(1) = PX(2) = ... = PX(6) = 1/6

In this example, it matches up to what we did with the random variables. It does have a different meaning. Your probability distribution is more about the spectrum of events that can happen, while our random variable example is all about which variables are there. With the probability theory, the P(X) part is going to note that we are working with our probability distribution of the random variable X.

While you take a look at this example, you may notice that your distribution could have just one variable, or there could be two or more of these variables that show up at the same time. When this occurs, you will name it a joint distribution. To figure out this probability, you will need to figure out the variables on their own and combine them to see the results.

In able to see how this is going to work when it comes to two or more variables, let's have X be the random variable and the one that will be defined by the outcome you can get any time you throw the die. Then you can use Y to show us the random variable that will tell you what results occur if you decide to flip a coin. For this one, to make things easier, we are going to assign the heads side of the coin 1, and the tails side is going to be 0. This is used to help us figure out the probability distribution for each variable on their own and together.

We are going to denote this joint distribution as P(X, Y) and the probability of X as having an outcome of a and Y as having an outcome of b as either P(x =a, Y =b) or PX, Y(a,b).

Conditional Distribution

The next thing we need to bring into the mix with machine learning and statistics is the idea of the conditional distribution. When we already know what the random variable distribution is all about, possibly because we already know the value of the second random variable, we can base the probability of one event on the outcome we can get with that second event. So, you will find that when you use this distribution, you will have the random variable be known as X when X -2 given that the variable of Y is going to be Y = b. When these are true, the following formula is going to help you to define and figure out what the variable is for both of the situations:

P(X = a|Y = b) = P(X = a, Y = b)/P(Y = b).

As you work through machine learning, there are going to be a few times when you may need to use conditional distributions. These can be useful tools depending on the system that you are designing, especially if you need to have the program reason with uncertainty.

Independence

And finally, when working with statistics and probability during machine learning, we need to consider independence. One of the variables that you can work with here is to figure out how much independence is inside the problem. When you work with these random variables, you are going to find out that they are going to be independent of what the other random variables are, as long as the distribution you have doesn't change if you take a new variable and try to add it into that equation.

To make this one work a bit better, you are going to need to work with a few assumptions in concerns to the data you are using with machine learning. This makes it a bit easier when you already know about independence. An excellent example to help us understand what this is all about is a training sample that uses j and I, and are independent of any underlying space when the label of sample I is unaffected by the features of sample j. No matter what one of the variables turns out, the other one is not going to see any change or be affected, if they are independent.

Think back to the example of the die and the coin flip. It doesn't matter what number shows up on the die. The coin is going to have its result. And the same can be said the other way around as well. The X random variable is always going to be independent of the Y variable. It doesn't matter the value of Y, but the following code needs to be true for it: $P(X) = P(X|Y)$.

In the case above, the values that come up for X and Y variables are dropped because, at this point, the values of these variables are not going to matter that much. But with the statement above, it is true for any value you provide to your X or Y, so it isn't going to matter what values are placed in this equation.

This phase went over a few of the things that you can do with the help of probability theory and statistics when you are working on machine learning. You can experiment with some of these to get the hang of what you can do using them, and then we can learn a few more algorithms that you can use later on.

Descriptive Statistics

The Excel Analysis ToolPak will include all of the tools described here. To get access to these tools you need to select the Data tab, then select the Analysis group and then choose Data Analysis. You might have to load the add-in program ToolPak if you aren't able to find the Data Analysis command.

Load and Activate the ToolPak

Some of you may already have the ToolPak in Excel, if you do, then go to the next step. For those who don't, let's look at how to get you started.

First, you will need to select the File tab and then select Options. After that, choose the Add-Ins category. If you have Excel 2007, you will need to click on the Microsoft Office Button, and then you will choose the Excel Options.

Also, if you would like to also have the Visual Basic for Application function for your ToolPak, you have the option of loading the ToolPak – VBA Add-in just like you loaded the ToolPak. Once you can access the Add-ins available box, you will choose the Analysis ToolPak – VBA.

Anova

The analysis tool, Anova, will provide you with other ways to analyze. The tools needed will depend on how many samples you collected and other factors you are interested in testing.

Anova: Single Factor

With this tool, you will be able to perform a simple analysis of variance on data that has at least two samples. This analysis will test your hypothesis that all of the samples come from the same distribution against the other theories that believe that the distributions aren't the same for every single one of your samples. If you only have a couple of samples, then you could choose the function T.Test. If you have over two samples, there aren't any convenient generalizations of T.Test; at this point, you can choose the Single Factor Anova model.

Anova: Two-Factor with Replication

When the data can be classified across two dimensions, this is the best tool to use. A great example will be if you have an experiment that measures different plant's height. You can give the plants different fertilizers, for this example, we will call them A, B, and C, and they may even be kept at various temperatures, such as high and low. For every one of the six possible pairs of temperature and fertilizer, you would have an equal amount of plant height observations. When you use the tool, you will be able to test:

- Whether the plant's height for the various temperatures comes from the same population; in this analysis, the fertilizer brands would be ignored.

- Whether the plant's height for the various fertilizers come from the same population; for this analysis, the temperatures would be ignored.

No matter if you are looking at the effects of the different temperatures or the different fertilizer brands, the six samples that represent each of the pair's values come from some group. The other hypothesis would be that there are effects caused by the specific temperature or fertilizer pairs about and over the difference that are only based on temperature or fertilizer.

Python Programming

Anova: Two-Factor without Replication

When you have data put into two sections just like in the Two-Fact with Replication, then this is a helpful analysis tool. But it will assume that you only have one observation for each of your pairs, in the previous example, it would be each of the temperature and fertilizer pairs.

Correlation

The Pearson and Correl worksheet functions will both come up with the correlation coefficient between the measurements of each of the variables have been observed for each of the different subjects. If there are missing observations for your subjects, it will cause the subject to be ignored during the analysis process. A particularly useful tool is the Correlation analysis tool when you have over two variables for every subject. It will give you a table, which is a correlation matrix; this will show you the Pearson value or Correl applied to all of your variables.

Like the covariance, the correlation coefficient is a way to measure how two variables may go together. Different from the covariance, the correlation coefficient will be proportioned for its value to be different from the units where the variables were shown. A good example would be if you have the variables of height and weight, the correlation coefficient value would not be changed if the weight amount gets changed to pounds from kilograms. Any correlation coefficient value would need to be anywhere from -1 and +1.

This tool is helpful when it comes to examining every pair of variables to figure out if the two will move at the same time. This means if a large value of one variable is often linked with the amount of the positive correlation, it doesn't matter if the small amount of a single variable gets linked with the large amount of the negative correlation, or if the value of each variable is typically not related with a correlation near zero.

Covariance

You can use the covariance and correlation tools in the same setting when you have a particular number of different measurement variables observed in a group of individuals. Both tools provide an output table, which is a matrix that will show covariance or correlation coefficient between every set of the measurement variables. One difference is the correlation coefficients get scaled to +1 and -1. When it comes to the corresponding covariance, they aren't scaled. Both of them provide the measures of how much the two variables vary together.

With the covariance tool, it will give you the amount of the function Covariance.P to be used for all of the pairs of variables. You can also directly use the Covariance.P instead of the Covariance tool when you only have two measurement variables. The diagonal entry of the output table in column I and row I is i-th variable's covariance. This represents the variables population variance that gets calculated by VAR.P.

The covariance tool can be used to look at every pair of variables to figure out if two variables move at the same time. This means if the big amount of one of the variables tends to be connected to the big amounts of the positive covariance, if the little amounts of a variable are connected to the negative covariance, or if the amount of both of them tends to be nothing.

Descriptive Statistics

This tool will give you an account of univariate statistics for all of the information that is in the range of input, as long as there is information on the variability and the tendency of the information.

Exponential Smoothing

This tool will predict an amount based on the prediction of a previous time and adjust for errors that occurred in the previous prediction. This tool makes use of the smoothing constant of a magnitude of this helps to determine how strong the forecasts tend to respond to the errors that happened in the previous forecast.

Keep in mind that the values of .2 to .3 are smoothing constants. This amount shows you that the current prediction needs to be changed to 20% to 30% to take into account the error of the previous forecast. A larger constant will yield a faster response, but they may give you erratic projections. A smaller constant may result in lags for a forecast value.

F-Test Two-Sample for Variances

This tool will perform a two-sample F-test so that you can compare two different population variances.

One example would be that you can use this tool on a sample of the times accrued during a swim competition for both teams. This tool will give you the results of the test for the prediction that the sample will be from the distribution that has the same variances; it puts it against the alternatives that a variance may not be equal to the distribution.

This tool will calculate the f value for an F-ratio. If f's value is near one, it tells you that the population variance is the same. If you have f < 1 "P(F ,= f) one-tail" it tells the odds of seeing F's value being lower than f when the population variance is the same.

"F Critical one-tail" will show you the critical value that is lower than one for the chosen level, Alpha. If f > 1, "P(F <= f) one-tail" it tells you that the odds of seeing the amount of the F are more than f when the population variance is the same. The "F Critical one-tail" will show you that the critical value is more than one for Alpha.

Histogram

With this tool, it can calculate cumulative and individual frequencies for the cell range of data bins and data. This will tell you the number of times that a number shows up in a set of data.

One example would be a class of 20 students; you will be able to figure the letter-grade distribution. A histogram will show you the boundaries and how many scores are between the current and lowest bound. The score that shows up the most often represents your data's mode.

If you are using Excel 2016, you will be able to create a Pareto or histogram chart.

- **Random number generation:** When you use this tool, you will get a range filled with independent random numbers, and are retrieved from one of many different distributions. The subject will be able to be characterized in a certain group with the odds of distribution. One example would be that you can find the heights of groups through normal distribution, or you may use the Bernoulli distribution for two answers that would be able to describe a coin-flip result.

- **Rank and percentile:** This tool will give you a table that provides you with the percentage and ordinal rank of every number in your dataset. You will be able to analyze the relative standing of the values within the dataset. This tool will make use of the worksheet functions Percentrank.Inc and Rank.EQ. If you're faced with values that are tied, use Rank.EQ because it will treat these values as the same rank, or the Rank.AVG can be used, which will give you the average of these tied values.

Regression

This tool will perform linear regressions by making use of the "least squares method" to add a line to your observation set. You will be able to analyze how independent variables affect dependent variables. If you wanted to see how the performance of an athlete is affected by things like weight, age, and height, you would be able to divide up shares in the measurement of performance to all of the information based on the performance data set, and you can use the results to predict how an untested athlete could perform.

Sampling

This tool will give you a group sample by reading the input range as a population. If you have a large population that is too big to chart or process, you will be able to make use of a representative sample. A sample can also be made to have only the value of a certain cycle area if you think you have periodic data. If you have an input range of quarterly sales, you can use a sample of the periodic rate of four, and it would add the value of this quarter into the output section.

Data Science Algorithms and Models

The algorithms used in data science can be divided into several categories, mainly supervised learning, unsupervised learning, and to some degree semi-supervised learning.

As the name suggests, supervised learning is aided by human interaction as the data scientist is required to provide the input and output in order to obtain a result from the predictions that are performed during the training process. Once the training is complete, the algorithm will use what it learned to apply to new, but similar data.

We are going to focus on this type of learning algorithm. However, take note that their purpose is divided based on the problems they need to solve. Mainly there are two distinct categories, namely regression and classification. In the case of regression problems, your target is a numeric value, while in classification it is a class or a label. To make things clearer, an example of a regression task is determining the average value of houses in a given city. A classification task, on the other hand, is supposed to take certain data like the petal and sepal length, and based on that information determine which is the species of a flower.

With that in mind, let's start by discussing regression algorithms and how to work with them.

Regression

In data science, many tasks are resolved with the help of regression techniques. However, a regression can also be categorized into two different branches, which are linear regression and logistic regression. Each one of them is used to solve different problems. However, both of them are a perfect choice for prediction analyses because of the high accuracy of the results.

The purpose of linear regression is to shape a prediction value out of a set of unrelated variables. This means that if you need to discover the relation between a number of variables you can apply a linear regression algorithm to do the work for you. However, this isn't its main use. Linear regression algorithms are used for regression tasks. Keep in mind that logistic regression is not used to solve regression problems as the name suggests. Instead, it is used for classification tasks.

With that being said, we are going to start by implementing a linear regression algorithm on the Boston housing dataset, which is freely available and even included in the Scikit-learn library. This dataset contains 506 samples, with 13 features and a numerical type target. We are going to break it into two sections, a training and a testing set. There are no rules set in stone regarding the ratio of the split; however, it is generally accepted that it is best to keep the training set with a 70%–80% data distribution and save 20%–30% for the testing process.

K-Nearest Neighbors

This algorithm is one of the easiest ones to work with; however, it can solve some of the most challenging classification problems. The k-nearest neighbor algorithm can be used in various scenarios that require anything from compressing data to processing financial data. It is one of the most commonly used supervised machine learning algorithms and you should do your best to practice your implementation technique.

The basic idea behind the algorithm is the fact that you should explore relation between two different training observations. For instance, we will call them x and y, and if you have the input value of x, you can already predict the value of y. The way this works is by calculating the distance of a data point in relation to other data points. The k-nearest point is selected based on this distance and it is assigned to a specific class.

To demonstrate how to implement this algorithm we are going to work with a much larger dataset than before; however, we will not use everything in it. Once again, we are going to rely on the Scikit-learn library in order to gain access to a dataset known as the MNIST handwritten digits dataset. In fact, a database that holds roughly 70,000 images of handwritten digits that are distributed in a training set with 60,000 images and a test set with 10,000 images. However, as already mentioned, we are not going to use the entire dataset because that would take too long for this demonstration. Instead, we will limit ourselves to 1000 samples. Let's get started:

In:

```
from sklearn.utils import shuffle
from sklearn.datasets import
from sklearn.cross_validation import train_test_split
import pickle

mnist = pickle.load(open( "mnist.pickle", "rb" ))
mnist.data, mnist.target = shuffle(mnist.data, mnist.target)
```

As usual, we first import the dataset and the tools we need. However, you will notice one additional step here, namely object serialization. This means we converted an object to a different format so that it can be used later but also reverted back to its original version if needed. This process is referred to as pickling and that is why we have the seemingly out of place pickle module imported. This will allow us to communicate objects through a network if needed. Now, let's cut through the dataset until we have only 1000 samples:

```
        mnist.data = mnist.data[:1000]
        mnist.target = mnist.target[:1000]

        X_train, X_test, y_train, y_test = train_test_split(mnist.data,
        mnist.target, test_size=0.8, random_state=0)
```

In:

```
        from sklearn.neighbors import KNeighborsClassifier
        # KNN: K=10, default measure of Euclidean distance
        clf = KNeighborsClassifier(3)
        clf.fit(X_train, y_train)
        y_pred = clf.predict(X_test)
```

Now let's see the report with the accuracy metrics like earlier:

In:

```
        from sklearn.metrics import classification_report
        print (classification_report(y_test, y_pred))
```

And here are the results:

Out:

	precision	recall	f1-score	support
0.0	0.68	0.90	0.78	79
1.0	0.66	1.00	0.79	95
2.0	0.83	0.50	0.62	76
3.0	0.59	0.64	0.61	85
4.0	0.65	0.56	0.60	75
5.0	0.76	0.55	0.64	80
6.0	0.89	0.69	0.77	70

7.0	0.76	0.83	0.79	76
8.0	0.91	0.56	0.69	77
9.0	0.61	0.75	0.67	87
avg / total	0.73	0.70	0.70	800

The results aren't the best, however, we have only implemented the "raw" algorithm without performing any kind of preparation operations that would clean and denote the data. Fortunately, the training speed was excellent even at this basic level. Remember, when working with supervised algorithms or any algorithms for that matter, you are always trading accuracy for processing speed or vice versa.

Support Vector Machines

The SVM is one of the most popular supervised learning algorithms due to its capability of solving both regressions as well as classification problems. In addition, it has the ability to identify outliers as well. This is one all-inclusive data science algorithm that you cannot miss. So what's so special about this algorithm?

First of all, support vector machines don't need much processing power in order to keep up with the prediction accuracy. This algorithm, however, is in a league of its own and you won't have to worry too much about sacrificing training speed for the accuracy or the other way around. Furthermore, support vector machines can be used to eliminate some of the noise as well while performing the regression or classification tasks.

This type of algorithm has many real-world applications and that is why it is important for you to understand its implementation. It is used in facial recognition software, text classification, handwriting recognition software, and so on. However, the basic concept behind it involves the distance between the nearest points where a hyperplane is selected from the margin between a number of support vectors. Take note that what is known as a hyperplane here is the object that divides the information space for the purpose of classification.

To put all of this theory in an application, we are going to rely on the Scikit-learn library once again. The algorithm will be implemented in such a way to demonstrate the accuracy of the prediction in the case of identifying real banknotes. We mentioned earlier that support vector machines are effective when it comes to image classification; therefore this algorithm is perfectly suited for our goals. What we need to solve in this example is a simple binary classification problem because we need to train the algorithm to determine whether the banknote is valid or not.

The bill will be described using several attributes. Keep in mind that unlike the other classification algorithms, a support vector machine determines its decision limit by defining the maximum distance between the data points which are nearest to the relevant classes. However, we aren't looking to limit the decision; we just want to find the best one. The nearest points in this best decision are what we refer to as support vectors. With that being said, let's import a new dataset and several tools:

```
import numpy as np
import pandas as pd
import matplotlib.pyplot as plt

dataset = pd.read_csv ("bank_note.csv")
```

As usual, the first step is learning more about the data we are working with. Let's learn how many rows and columns we have and then obtain the data from the first five rows only:

```
print (dataset.shape)
print (dataset.head())
```

Here's the result:

	Variance	Skewness	Curtosis	Entropy	Class
0	3.62160	8.6661	-2.8073	-0.44699	0
1	4.454590	8.1674	-2.4586	-1.46210	0
2	3.86600	-2.6383	1.9242	0.10645	0
3	3.45660	9.5228	-4.0112	-3.59440	0
4	0.32924	-4.4552	4.5718	-0.98880	0

Now we need to process this information in order to establish the training and testing sets. This means that we need to reduce the data to attributes and labels only:

```
x = dataset.drop ('Class', axis = 1)
y = dataset ['Class']
```

The purpose of this code is to store the column data as the x variable and then apply the drop function in order to avoid the class column so that we can store it inside a 'y' variable. By reducing the dataset to a collection of attributes and labels we can start defining the training and testing data sets. Split the data just like we did in all the earlier examples. Next, let's start implementing the algorithm.

Python Programming

We need Scikit-learn for this step because it contains the support vector machine algorithm; therefore, we can easily access it without requiring outside sources.

```
from sklearn.svm import SVC
svc_classifier = SVC (kernel = 'linear')
svc_classifier.fit (x_train, y_train)
pred_y = svc.classifier.predict(x_test)
```

Finally, we need to check the accuracy of our implementation. For this step, we are going to use a confusion matrix that will act as a table that displays the accuracy values of the classification's performance. You will see a number of true positives, true negatives, as well as false positives and false negatives. The accuracy value is determined from these values. With that being said, let's take a look at the confusion matrix and then print the classification report:

```
from sklearn.metric import confusion_matrix
print (confusion_matrix (y_test, pred_y)
```

This is the output:

[[160 1]

[1   113]]

Accuracy Score: 0.99

Now let's see the familiar classification report:

```
from sklearn.metrics import classification_report
print (classification_report(y_test, y_pred))
```

And here are the results of the report:

	precision	recall	f1-score	support
0.0	0.99	0.99	0.99	161
1.0	0.99	0.99	0.99	114
avg / total	0.99	0.99	0.99	275

Based on all of these metrics, we can determine that we obtained a very high accuracy with our implementation of the support vector machines. A score of 0.99 is almost as good as it can get; however, there is always room for improvement.

Indexing and Selecting Arrays

Array indexing is similar to List indexing with the same techniques of item selection and slicing (using square brackets). The methods are even more similar when the array is a vector.

Example:

In []:

```
# Indexing a vector array (values)
values
values [0] # grabbing 1st item
values [-1] # grabbing last item
values [1:3] # grabbing 2nd & 3rd item
values [3:8] # item 4 to 8
```

Out []:

> *array ([1.33534821, 1.73863505, 0.1982571, -0.47513784, 1.80118596, -1.73710743, -0.24994721, 1.41695744, -0.28384007, 0.58446065])*
>
> *1.3353482110285562*
>
> *0.5844606470172699*
>
> *array ([1.73863505, 0.1982571])*
>
> *array ([-0.47513784, 1.80118596, -1.73710743, -0.24994721, 1.41695744])*

The main difference between arrays and lists is in the broadcast property of arrays. When a slice of a list is assigned to another variable, any changes on that new variable does not affect the original list. This is seen in the example below:

In []:

```
num_list = list (range (11))   # list from 0-10
num_list                        # display list
list_slice = num_list [:4]     # first 4 items
list_slice                      # display slice
list_slice [:] = [5,7,9,3]     # Re-assigning elements
list_slice                      # display updated values
# checking for changes
if list_slice == num_list [:4]:
    print (' The list changed!')
else :
    print (' no changes in original list')
```

Out []:

```
[0, 1, 2, 3, 4, 5, 6, 7, 8, 9, 10]

[0, 1, 2, 3]

[5, 7, 9, 3]

No changes in the original list.
```

However, for arrays a change in the slice of an array also updates or broadcasts to the original array; thereby changing its values.

In []:

```
# Checking the broadcast feature of arrays
num_array = np.arrange (11)    # array from 0-10
num_array                      # display array
array_slice = num_array [:4]   # first 4 items
array_slice                    # display slice
array_slice [:] = [5,7,9,3]    # Re-assigning elements
array_slice                    # display updated values
num_array
```

Out []:

```
array ([ 0, 1, 2, 3, 4, 5, 6, 7, 8, 9, 10])

array ([0, 1, 2, 3])

array ([5, 7, 9, 3])

array ([ 5, 7, 9, 3, 4, 5, 6, 7, 8, 9, 10])
```

This happens because Python tries to save memory allocation by allowing slices of an array to be like shortcuts or links to the actual array. This way it doesn't have to allocate a separate memory location to it. This is especially ingenious in the case of large arrays whose slices can also take up significant memory. However, to take up a slice of an array without broadcast, you can create a 'slice of a copy' of the array. The array. copy () method is called to create a copy of the original array.

In []:

```
# Here is an array allocation without broadcast
num_array     # Array from the last example

# copies the first 4 items of the array copy
array_slice = num_array.copy() [:4]
array_slice
# display array
array_slice [:] = 10
# re-assign array
array_slice
# display updated values
num_array
```

Out []:

```
array ([ 5, 7, 9, 3, 4, 5, 6, 7, 8, 9, 10])

array ([5, 7, 9, 3])

array ([10, 10, 10, 10])

array ([ 5, 7, 9, 3, 4, 5, 6, 7, 8, 9, 10])
```

Notice that the original array remains unchanged.

For two-dimensional arrays or matrices, the same indexing and slicing methods work. However, it is always easy to consider the first dimension as the rows and the other as the columns. To select any item or a slice of items, the index of the rows and columns are specified. Let us illustrate this with a few examples:

Example: Grabbing elements from a matrix

Python Programming

There are two methods for grabbing elements from a matrix: array_name[row][col] or array_name [row, col].

In []:

```
# Here is an array allocation without broadcast
```

```
# Creating the matrix
matrix = np. array (([5,10,15], [20,25,30], [35,40,45]))

matrix      #display matrix
matrix [1]    # Grabbing second row
matrix [2][0] # Grabbing 35
matrix [0:2] # Grabbing first 2 rows
matrix [2,2] # Grabbing 45
```

Out []:

```
array ([[ 5, 10, 15],
       [20, 25, 30],
       [35, 40, 45]])

array ([20, 25, 30])

35

array ([[ 5, 10, 15],
       [20, 25, 30]])

45
```

Tip: It is recommended to use the array_name [row, col] method; it saves typing and is more compact. This will be the convention for the rest of this section.

To grab columns, we specify a slice of the row and column. Let us try to grab the second column in the matrix and assign it to a variable column_slice.

In []:

```
# Grabbing the second column
column_slice = matrix [: 1:2] # Assigning to variable column_slice
 # Creating the matrix
```

Out []:

```
array ([[10],
       [25],
       [40]])
```

Let us consider what happened here. To grab the column slice, we first specify the row before the comma. Since our column contains elements in all rows, we need all the rows to be included in our selection, hence the ':' sign for all. Alternatively, we could use '0:,' which might be easier to understand. After selecting the row, we then choose the column by specifying a slice from '1:2', which tells Python to grab from the second item up to (but not including) the third item. Remember, Python indexing starts from zero.

Exercise: Try to create a larger array, and use these indexing techniques to grab certain elements from the array. For example, here is a larger array:

In []:

Python Programming

```
# 5 × 10 Array of even numbers between 0 and 100.
large_array = np. arrange (0,100,2). reshape (5,10)
large_array    # show
```

Out []:

```
array ([[ 0, 2, 4, 6, 8, 10, 12, 14, 16, 18],
       [20, 22, 24, 26, 28, 30, 32, 34, 36, 38],
       [40, 42, 44, 46, 48, 50, 52, 54, 56, 58],
       [60, 62, 64, 66, 68, 70, 72, 74, 76, 78],
       [80, 82, 84, 86, 88, 90, 92, 94, 96, 98]])
```

Tip: Try grabbing single elements and rows from random arrays you create. After getting very familiar with this, try selecting columns. The point is to try as many combinations as possible to get you familiar with the approach. If the slicing and indexing notations are confusing, try to revisit the section under list or string slicing and indexing.

Click this link to revisit the examples on slicing: List indexing

Conditional selection

Consider a case where we need to extract certain values from an array that meet a Boolean criterion. NumPy offers a convenient way of doing this without having to use loops.

Example: Using a conditional selection

Consider this array of odd numbers between 0 and 20. Assuming we need to grab elements above 11. We first have to create the conditional array that selects this:

In []:

```
odd_array = np.arrange (1,20,2)   # Vector of odd numbers
odd_array                          # Show vector
bool_array = odd_array > 11       # Boolean conditional array
bool_array
```

Out []:

```
array ([ 1, 3, 5, 7, 9, 11, 13, 15, 17, 19])

array ([False, False, False, False, False, False, True, True, True, True])
```

Notice how the bool_array evaluates to True at all instances where the elements of the odd_array meet the Boolean criterion.

The Boolean array itself is not usually so useful. To return the values that we need, we will pass the Boolean_array into the original array to get our results.

In []:

```
useful_Array = odd_array[bool_array]  # The values we want
useful_Array
```

Out []:

```
array ([13, 15, 17, 19])
```

Now, that is how to grab elements using conditional selection. However, there is a more compact way of doing this. It is the same idea, but it reduces typing.

Instead of first declaring a Boolean_array to hold our truth values, we just pass the condition into the array itself, as we did for useful_array.

In []:
```
# This code is more compact
compact = odd_array[odd_array>11] # One line
compact
```

Out []:
```
array ([13, 15, 17, 19])
```

See how we achieved the same result with just two lines? It is recommended to use this second method, as it saves coding time and resources. The first method helps explain how it all works. However, we would be using the second method for all other instances in this book.

Exercise: The conditional selection works on all arrays (vectors and matrices alike). Create a two 3 × 3 array of elements greater than 80 from the 'large_array' given in the last exercise.

Hint: use the reshape method to convert the resulting array into a 3 × 3 matrix.

NumPy Array Operations

Finally, we will be exploring basic arithmetical operations with NumPy arrays. These operations are not unlike that of integer or float Python lists.

Array – Array Operations

In NumPy, arrays can operate with and on each other using various arithmetic operators. Things like the addition of two arrays, division, etc.

Example:

In []:

```
# Array - Array Operations
# Declaring two arrays of 10 elements
Array1 = np. arrange (10). reshape (2,5)
Array2 = np. random. rind (10). reshape (2,5)
Array1; Array2          # Show the arrays

# Addition
Array_sum = Array1 + Array2
Array_sum               # show result array

#Subtraction
Array_minus = Array1 - Array2
Array_minus             # Show array

# Multiplication
Array_product = Array1 * Array2
Array_product           # Show

# Division
Array_divide = Array1 / Array2
Array_divide            # Show
```

Out []:

> *array ([[0, 1, 2, 3, 4],*
> *[5, 6, 7, 8, 9]])*
>
> *array ([[2.09122638, 0.45323217, -0.50086442, 1.00633093, 1.24838264],*
> *[1.64954711, -0.93396737, 1.05965475, 0.78422255, -1.84595505]])*
>
> *array ([[2.09122638, 1.45323217, 1.49913558, 4.00633093, 5.24838264],*
> *[6.64954711, 5.06603263, 8.05965475, 8.78422255, 7.15404495]])*
>
> *array ([[-2.09122638, 0.54676783, 2.50086442, 1.99366907, 2.75161736],*
> *[3.35045289, 6.93396737, 5.94034525, 7.21577745, 10.84595505]])*
>
> *array ([[0., 0.45323217, -1.00172885, 3.01899278, 4.99353055],*
> *[8.24773555, -5.60380425, 7.41758328, 6.27378038, -16.61359546]])*
>
> *array ([[0., 2.20637474, -3.99309655, 2.9811267, 3.20414581],*
> *[3.03113501, -6.42420727, 6.60592516, 10.20118591, -4.875525]])*

Each of the arithmetic operations performed are element-wise. However, the division operations require extra care. In Python, most arithmetic errors in code throw a run-time error, which helps in debugging. For NumPy, however, the code could run with a warning issued.

Array – Scalar operations

Also, NumPy supports scalar with Array operations. A scalar in this context is just a single numeric value of either integer or float type. The scalar – Array operations are also element-wise, by virtue of the broadcast feature of NumPy arrays.

Example:

In []:

```python
#Scalar- Array Operations
new_array = np.arrange(0,11)    # Array of values from 0-10
print('New_array')
new_array                # Show
Sc = 100                 # Scalar value

# let us make an array with a range from 100 - 110 (using +)
add_array = new_array + Sc    # Adding 100 to every item
print('\nAdd_array')
add_array                # Show
# Let us make an array of 100s (using -)
centurion = add_array - new_array
print('\nCenturion')
centurion                # Show
# Let us do some multiplication (using *)
multiplex = new_array * 100
print('\nMultiplex')
multiplex                # Show
# division [take care], let us deliberately generate
# an error. We will do a divide by Zero.
err_vec = new_array / new_array
print('\nError_vec')
err_vec
# Show
New_array
```

Out []:

> *New_array*
> array ([0, 1, 2, 3, 4, 5, 6, 7, 8, 9, 10])
>
> *Add_array*
> array ([100, 101, 102, 103, 104, 105, 106, 107, 108, 109, 110])
>
> *Centurion*
> array ([100, 100, 100, 100, 100, 100, 100, 100, 100, 100, 100])
>
> *Multiplex*
> array ([0, 100, 200, 300, 400, 500, 600, 700, 800, 900, 1000])
>
> *Error_vec*
> C:\Users\Oguntuase\Anaconda3\lib\site-packages\ipykernel_launcher.py:27:
> RuntimeWarning: invalid value encountered in true_divide
>
> array ([nan, 1., 1., 1., 1., 1., 1., 1., 1., 1.])

Neural Network

A widely used approach in machine learning, the employment of artificial neural network is inspired by the brain system of humans. The objective of neural networks is replicating how the human brain learns. The neural network system is an ensemble of input and output layers and a hidden layer that transforms the input layer into useful information to the output layer. Usually, several hidden layers are implemented in an artificial neural network. The figure below presents an example of a neural network system composed of 2 hidden layers:

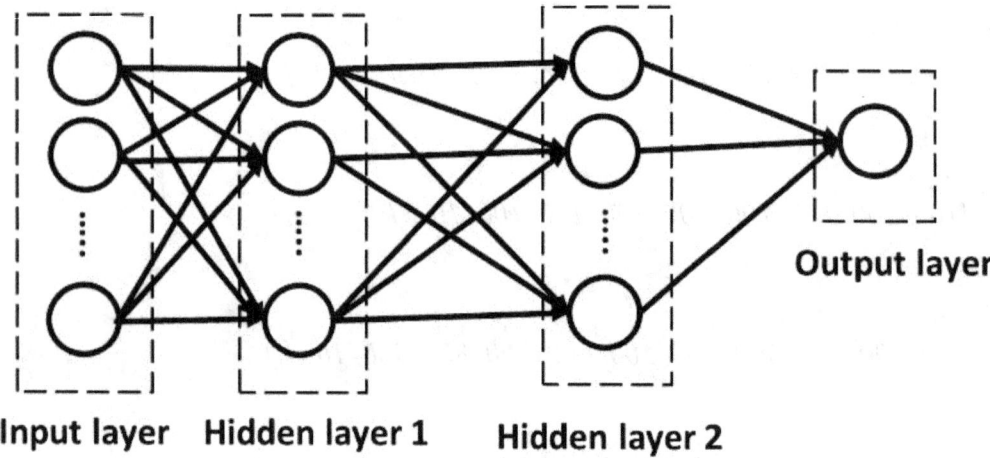

Input layer   Hidden layer 1   Hidden layer 2

Example of an artificial neural network

Before going further and explaining how neural networks work, let's first define what is a neuron. A neuron is simply a mathematical equation expressed as the sum of the weighted inputs. Let's consider X={x1, x2,....xM} a vector of N inputs; the neuron is a linear combination of all inputs defined as follows:

F(X={x1, x2,....xM})=w1x1+w2x2+....+wMxM;

With w1, w2,...wM is the weights assigned to each input. The function F can also be represented as:

F(X) =WX,

With W a weight matrix and X a vector of data. The second formulation is very convenient when programming a neural network model. The weights are determined during the training procedure. In fact, training an artificial neural network means finding the optimal weights W that provide the most accurate output.

To each neuron, an activation function is applied the resulted weighted sum of inputs X. The role of the activation function is deciding whether the neuron should be activated or not according to the model's prediction. This process is applied to each layer of the network. In the next sub-phases, we will discuss in detail the role and types of activation functions as well as the different types of neural networks.

What Is an Activation Function and Its Role in Neural Network Models?

Activation functions are formulated as mathematical functions. These functions are a crucial component of an artificial neural network model. For each neuron, an activation function is associated. The activation function decides whether to activate the neuron or not. For instance, let's consider the output from a neuron, which is:

$Y = \sum$ (weight*input) +bias.

The output Y can be of any value. The neuron does not have any information on the reasonable range of values that Y can take. For this purpose, the activation function is implemented in the neural network to check Y values and make a decision on whether the neural connections should consider this neuron activated or not.

There are different types of activation functions. The most instinctive function is the step function. This function sets a threshold and decides to activate or not activate a neuron if it exceeds a certain threshold. In other words, the output of this function is 1 if Y is greater than a threshold and 0 otherwise. Formally, the activation function is:

F='activated' or F=1; if Y> threshold

F='not-activated' or F=0; otherwise.

This activation function can be used for a classification problem where the output should be yes or no (i.e., 0 or 1). However, it has some drawbacks. For example, let's consider a set of several categories (i.e., class1, class2, ..., etc.) to which input may belong to. If this activation function is used and more than one neuron is activated, the output will be 1 for all neurons. In this case, it is hard to distinguish between the classes and decide which class the input belongs to because all neuron outputs are 1. In short, the step function does not support multiple output values and classification into several classes.

The linear activation function, unlike the step function, provides a range of activation values. It computes an output that is proportional to the input. Formally: $F(X)=WX$, where X is the input.

This function supports several outputs rather than just 1 or 0 values. This function, because it is linear, does not support backpropagation for model training.

Backpropagation is the process that relies on function derivative or gradient to update the parameters, in particular, the weights. The derivative (i.e., gradient) of the linear activation function is a constant equal to W and is not related to changes in the input X. Therefore, it does not provide information on which weights applied to the input can give accurate predictions.

Moreover, all layers can be reduced to one layer when using the linear function. The fact that all layers are using a linear function, the final layer is a linear function of the first layer. So, no matter how many layers are used in the neural network, they are equivalent to the first layer, and there is no point in using multiple layers. A neural network with multiple layers connected with a linear activation function is just a linear regression model that cannot support the complexity of input data.

The majority of neural networks use non-linear activation functions because, in the majority of real-world applications, relations between the output and the input features are non-linear. The non-linear functions allow the neural network to map complex patterns between the inputs and the outputs. They also allow the neural network to learn the complex process that governs complex data or high dimension data such as images, audios, among others. The non-linear functions allow overcoming the drawbacks of linear functions and step functions. They support backpropagation (i.e., the derivative is not a constant and depends on the changes of the input) and stacking several layers (i.e., the combination of non-linear functions is non-linear). Several non-linear functions exist and can be used within a neural network. In this phase, we are going to cover the most commonly used non-linear activation functions in machine learning applications.

The sigmoid function is one of the most used activation functions within an artificial neural network. Formally, a sigmoid function is equal to the inverse of the sum of 1 and the exponential of inputs: $F(X) = 1/(1+\exp(-X))$

Outputs of a sigmoid function are bounded by 0 and 1. More precisely, the outputs take any value between 0 and 1 and provide clear predictions. In fact, when the X is greater than 2 or lower than -2, the value of Y is close to the edge of the curve (i.e., closer to 0 or 1).

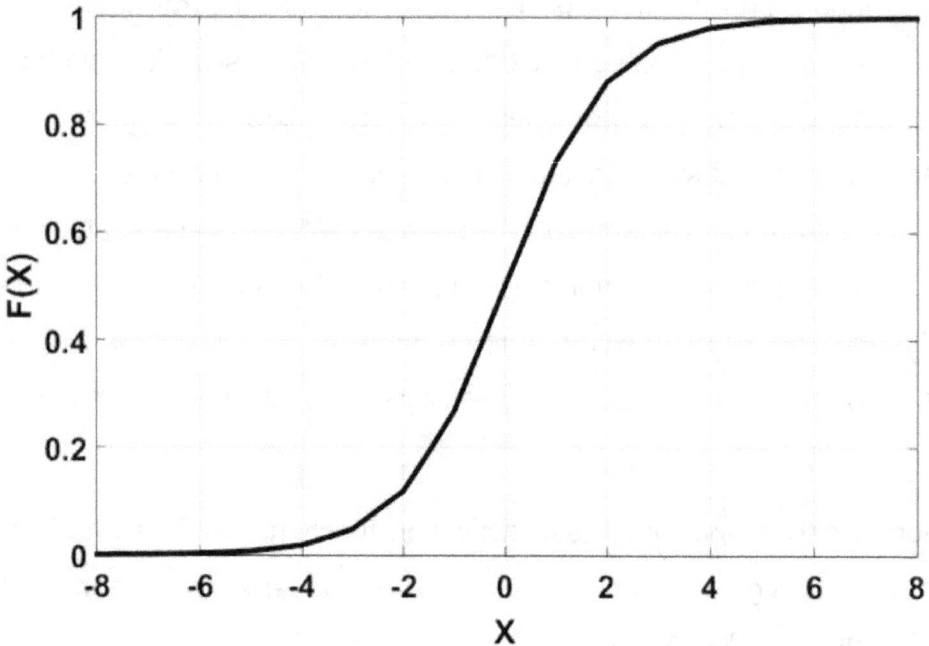

Sigmoid activation function

The disadvantage of this activation function, as we can see from the figure above, is the small change in the output for input values under -4 and above 4. This problem is called 'vanishing gradient,' which means that the gradient is very small on horizontal extremes of the curve. This makes a neural network using the sigmoid function, learning very slowly when they approach the edges and computationally expensive.

The tanh function is another activation function used that is similar to the sigmoid function. The mathematical formulation of this function is: F(X)=tanh(X)=[2/(1+exp(-2X)]-1.

This function is a scaled sigmoid function. Therefore, it has the same characteristics as the sigmoid function. However, the outputs of this function range between -1 and 1, and the gradient are more pronounced than the gradient of the sigmoid function. Unlike the sigmoid function, the tanh function is zero-centered, which makes it very useful for inputs with negative, neutral, and positive values. The drawback of this function, as for the sigmoid function, is the vanishing gradient issue and computationally expensive.

The Rectified Linear Unit function, as the ReLu function, is also a widely used activation function, which is computationally efficient. This function is efficient and allows the neural network to converge quickly compared to the sigmoid and tanh function because it uses simple mathematical formulations. ReLu returns X as output if X is positive or 0 otherwise. Formally, this activation function is formulated as $F(X)=max(0,X)$.

This activation function is not bounded and takes values from 0 to +inf. Although it has a similar shape as a linear function (i.e., this function is equal to identity for positive values), the ReLu function has a derivative. The drawback of the ReLu is that the derivative (i.e., the gradient) is 0 when the inputs are negative. This means that as far as linear functions, the backpropagation cannot be processed, and the neural network cannot learn unless the inputs are greater than 0. This aspect of the ReLu, gradient equal to 0 when the inputs are negative, is called the dying ReLu problem.

To prevent the dying ReLu problem, two ReLu variations can be used, namely the Leaky ReLu function and the Parametric ReLu function. The Leakey ReLu function returns as output the maximum of X and X by 0.1. In other words, the leaky ReLu is equal to the identity function when X is greater than 0 and is equal to the product of 0.1 and X when X is less than zero. This function is provided as follows: $F(X)=max(0.1*X, X)$

This function has a small positive gradient that o.1 when X has negative values, which makes this function support backpropagation for negative values. However, it may not provide a consistent prediction for these negative values.

The parametric ReLu function is similar to the Leaky ReLu function that takes the gradient as a parameter to the neural network to define the output when X is negative. The mathematical formulation of this function is as follows: F(X)=max (aX, X)

There are other variations of the ReLu function such as the exponential linear ReLu. This function, unlike the other variations of the ReLu the Leaky ReLu and parametric ReLu, has a log curve for negative values of X instead of the linear curves like the Leaky ReLu and the parametric ReLu functions. The downside of this function is it saturates for large negative values of X. Other variations exist which rely on the same concept of defining a gradient greater than 0 when X has negative values.

The Softmax function is another type of activation function used differently. This function is usually applied only to the output layer when a classification of the inputs into several different classes is needed. In fact, the Softmax function supports several classes and provides the probability of input to belong to a specific class. It normalizes outputs of every category between 0 and 1 then divides by their sum to provide that probability. Given all these activation functions, where each one has its pros and cons, the question now which one should be used in a neural network? The answer is simply that having a better understanding of the problem at hand will help guide into a specific activation function, especially if the characteristics of the function being approximated are known beforehand. For instance, a sigmoid function is a good choice for a classification problem. In case the nature of the function being approximated is unknown, it is highly recommended to start with a ReLu function than try other activation function. Overall, the ReLu function works well for a wide range of applications. It is an ongoing research, and you may try your own activation function.

Deep Learning vs. Machine Learning

Before we begin, it is important you remind yourself of the basic definitions or explanations of these two subjects. Machine learning is a branch of artificial intelligence that uses algorithms to teach machines how to learn. Further from the algorithms, the machine learning models need input and output data from which they can learn through interaction with different users.

When building such models, it is always advisable to ensure that you build a scalable project that can take new data when applicable and use it to keep training the model and boost its efficiency. An efficient machine learning model should be able to self-modify without necessarily requiring your input and still provide the correct output. It learns from a structured data available and keeps updating itself.

Deep learning is a class of machine learning that uses the same algorithms and functions used in machine learning. However, deep learning introduces layered computing beyond the power of algorithms. Algorithms in deep learning are used in layers, with each layer interpreting data in a different way. The algorithm network used in deep learning is referred to as artificial neural networks.

The name artificial neural networks gives us the closest iteration of what happens in deep learning frameworks. The goal here is to try and mimic the way the human brain functions by focusing on the neural networks. Experts in deep learning sciences have studied and referenced different studies on the human brain over the years, which has helped spearhead research into this field.

Problem Solving Approaches

Let's consider an example to explain the difference between deep learning and machine learning.

Say you have a database that contains photos of trucks and bicycles. How can you use machine learning and deep learning to make sense of this data? At first glance, what you will see is a group of trucks and bicycles. What if you need to identify photos of bicycles separately from trucks using these two frameworks?

To help your machine learning algorithm identify the photos of trucks and bicycles based on the categories requested, you must first teach it what these photos are about. How does the machine learning algorithm figure out the difference? After all, they almost look alike.

The solution is in a structured data approach. First, you will label the photos of bicycles and trucks in a manner that defines different features that are unique to either of these items. This is sufficient data for your machine learning algorithm to learn from. Based on the input labels, it will keep learning and refine its understanding of the difference between trucks and bicycles as it encounters more data. From this simple illustration, it will keep searching through millions of other data it can access to tell the difference between trucks and bicycles.

How Do We Solve This Problem in Deep Learning?

The approach in deep learning is different from what we have done in machine learning. The benefit here is that in deep learning, you do not need any labeled or structured data to help the model identify trucks from bicycles.

The artificial neural networks will identify the image data through the different algorithm layers in the network. Each of the layers will identify and define a specific feature in the photos. This is the same method that our brains use when we try to solve some problems.

Generally, the brain considers a lot of possibilities, ruling out all the wrong ones before settling on the correct one. Deep learning models will pass queries through several hierarchical processes to find the solution. At each identification level, the deep neural networks recognize some identifiers that help in distinguishing bicycles from trucks.

This is the simplest way to understand how these two systems work. However, both deep learning and machine learning might not necessarily be applicable methods to tell these photos apart. As you learn about the differences between these two fields, you must remember you have to define the problem correctly before you can choose the best approach to implement in solving it. You will learn how to choose the right approach at a later stage in your journey into machine learning, which has been covered in the advanced books in this series.

From the example illustrated above, we can see that machine learning algorithms need structured data to help them tell the difference between trucks and bicycles. From this information, they can then produce the correct output after identifying the classifiers.

However, in deep learning, your model can identify images of the trucks and bicycles by passing information through several data processing layers in its framework. There is no need for structured data. To make the correct prediction, deep learning frameworks depend on the output provided at every data processing layer. This information builds up and presents the final outcome. In this case, it rules out all possibilities to remain with the only credible solution.

From our illustrations above, we have learned some important facts that will help you distinguish deep learning from machine learning as you learn over the years. We can summarize this in the following points:

- **Data presentation:** The primary difference between machine learning and deep learning is evident in the way we introduce data into the respective models. With machine learning models, you will almost always need to use structured data. However, in deep learning, the networks depend on artificial neural network layers to identify unique features that help to identify the data.

- **Algorithms and human intervention:** The emphasis of machine learning is to learn from interacting with different inputs and use patterns. From such interaction, machine learning models can produce better output the longer it learns, and the more interaction it receives.

To aid this cause, you must also try to provide as much new data as possible.

When you realize that the output presented is not what you needed, you must retrain the machine learning model to deliver a better output. Therefore, for a system that should work without human intervention, you will still have to be present from time to time.

In deep learning, your presence is not needed. All the nested layers within the neural networks process data at different levels. In the process, however, the model might encounter errors and learn from them.

This is the same way that the human brain works. As you grow up, you learn a lot of important life skills through trial and error. By making mistakes, your brain learns the difference between positive and negative feedback, and you strive to achieve positive results whenever you can.

To be fair, even in deep learning, your input will still be required. You cannot confidently assume that the output will always be perfect. This particularly applies when your input data is insufficient for the kind of output you demand from the model.

The underlying factor here is that both machine learning and deep learning must use all the data. The quality of data you have will make a lasting impact on the results you get from these models. Speaking of data, you cannot just use any data you come across. To use either of these models effectively, you must learn how to inspect data and make sure you are using the correct format for the model you prefer.

Machine learning algorithms will often need labeled and structured data. For this reason, they are not the best option if you need to find solutions to sophisticated problems that need massive chunks of data.

In the example we used to identify trucks from bicycles, we tried to solve a very simple issue in a theoretical concept. In the real world, however, deep learning models are applied in more complex models. If you think about the processes involved, from the concepts to hierarchical data handling and the different number of layers that data must pass through, using deep learning models to solve simple problems would be a waste of resources.

While all these classes of AI need data to help in conducting the intelligence we require, deep learning models need significantly wider access to data than machine learning algorithms. This is important because deep learning algorithms must prove beyond a reasonable doubt that the output is perfect before it is passed. Deep learning models can easily identify differences and concepts in the data processing layers for neural networks only when they have been exposed to millions of data points. This helps to rule out all other possibilities. However, in the case of machine learning, the models can learn through criteria that are already predetermined.

Different Use Cases

Having seen the difference between machine learning and deep learning, where can these two be applied in the real world? Deep learning is a credible solution in case you deal with massive amounts of data. In this case, you will need to interpret and make decisions from such data; hence you need a model that is suitable given your resource allocation.

Deep learning models are also recommended when dealing with problems that are too complicated to solve using machine learning algorithms. Beyond this, it is important to realize that deep learning models usually have a very high resource demand. Therefore, you should consider deep learning models when you have the necessary financial muscle and resource allocation to obtain the relevant programs and hardware.

Machine learning is a feasible solution when working with structured data that can be used to train different machine learning algorithms. There is a lot of learning involved before the algorithms can perform the tasks requested.

You can also use machine learning to enjoy the benefits of artificial intelligence without necessarily implementing a full-scale artificial intelligence model.

Machine learning algorithms are often used to help or speed up automation processes in businesses and industrial processes. Some common examples of machine learning models in use include advertising, identity verifiers, information processing, and marketing. These should help your business position itself better in the market against the competition.

Application of Machine Learning Using Scikit-Learn Library

To understand how Scikit-Learn library is used in the development of a machine learning algorithm, let us use the "Sales_Win_Loss data set from IBM's Watson repository" containing data obtained from sales campaign of a wholesale supplier of automotive parts. We will build a machine learning model to predict which a sales campaign will be a winner and which will incur a loss.

The data set can be imported using Pandas and explored using Pandas techniques such as "head (), tail (), and dtypes ()." The plotting techniques from "Seaborn" will be used to visualize the data and to process the data Scikit-Learn's preprocessing.

LabelEncoder ()" will be used and "train_test_split ()" to divide the data set into a training subset and testing subset.

To generate predictions from our data set, three different algorithms will be used namely, "Linear Support Vector Classification and K-nearest neighbor's classifier." To compare the performances of these algorithms Scikit-Learn library technique "accuracy_score" will be used. The performance score of the models can be visualized using Scikit-Learn and "Yellowbrick" visualization.

Importing the Data Set

To import the "Sales_Win_Loss data set from IBM's Watson repository," the first step is importing the "Pandas" module using "import pandas as pd."

Then we leverage a variable URL as, "https://community.watsonanalytics.com/wp content/uploads/2015/04/WA_Fn-UseC_-Sales-Win-Loss.csv" to store the URL from which the data set will be downloaded.

Now, "read_csv () as sales_data = pd. read_csv(url)" technique will be used to read the above "csv or comma-separated values" file, which is supplied by the Pandas module. The csv file will then be converted into a Pandas data framework, with the return variable as "sales_data," where the framework will be stored.

For new 'Pandas' users, the "pd. read csv ()" technique in the code mentioned above will generate a tabular data structure called "data framework", where an index for each row is contained in the first column, and the label/name for each column in the first row are the initial column names acquired from the data set. In the above code snippet, the "sales data" variable results in a table depicted in the picture below.

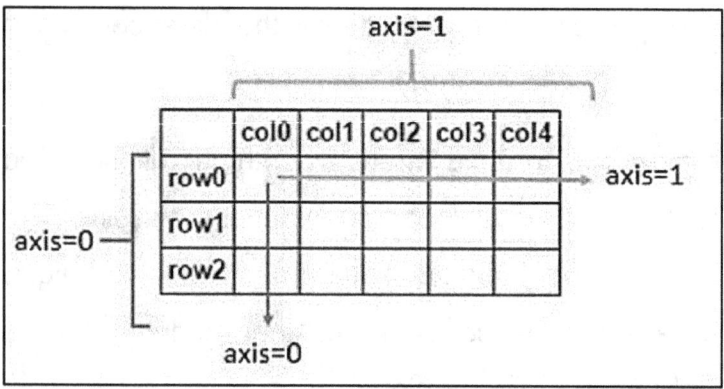

In the diagram above, the "row0, row1, row2" represent individual record index, and the "col0, col1, col2" represent the names for individual columns or features of the data set.

With this step, you have successfully stored a copy of the data set and transformed it into a "Pandas" framework!

Now, using the "head () as Sales_data. Head ()" technique, the records from the data framework can be displayed as shown below to get a "feel" of the information contained in the data set.

	opportunity number	supplies subgroup	supplies group	region	route to market	elapsed days in sales stage	opportunity result
0	1641984	Exterior Accessories	Car Accessories	Northwest	Fields Sales	76	Won
1	1658010	Exterior Accessories	Car Accessories	Pacific	Reseller	63	Loss
2	1674737	Motorcycle Parts	Performance & Non-auto	Pacific	Reseller	24	Won
3	1675224	Shelters & RV	Performance & Non-auto	Midwest	Reseller	16	Loss

Data Exploration

Now that we have our own copy of the data set, which has been transformed into a "Pandas" data frame, we can quickly explore the data to understand what information can be gathered from it and accordingly to plan a course of action.

In any ML project, data exploration tends to be a very critical phase. Even a fast data set exploration can offer us significant information that could be easily missed otherwise, and this information can propose significant questions that we can attempt to answer using our project.

Some third-party Python libraries will be used here to assist us with the processing of the data so we can efficiently use this data with the powerful algorithms of Scikit-Learn. The same "head ()" technique that we used to see some initial records of the imported data set in the earlier section can be used here. As a matter of fact, "(head)" is effectively capable of doing much more than displaying data records and customize the "head ()" technique to display only a selected records with commands like "sales_data.head(n=2)." This command will selectively display the first 2 records of the data set. At a quick glance, it's obvious that columns such as, Region" and "Supplies Group" contain string data, while columns such as "Opportunity Result," "Opportunity Number," etc., are comprised of integer values. It can also be seen that there are unique identifiers for each record in the' Opportunity Number' column.

Similarly, to display select records from the bottom of the table, the "tail() as sales_data.tail()" can be used.

To view the different data types available in the data set, the Pandas technique "dtypes() as sales_data.dtypes" can be used. With this information, the data columns available in the data framework can be listed with their respective data types. We can figure out, for example, that the column "Supplies Subgroup" is an "object" data type and that the column "Client Size by Revenue" is an "integer data type." So, we have an understanding of columns that either contains integer values or string data.

Data Visualization

At this point, we are through with basic data exploration steps, so we will not attempt to build some appealing plots to portray the information visually and discover other concealed narratives from our data set.

Of all the available Python libraries providing data visualization features; "Seaborn" is one of the best available options, so we will be using the same. Make sure that the python plots module provided by "Seaborn" has been installed on your system and ready to be used. Now follow the steps below generate the desired plot for the data set:

- **Step 1** – Import the "Seaborn" module with the command "import seaborn as sns."

- **Step 2** – Import the "Matplotlib" module with command "import matplotlib.pyplot as plt."

- **Step 3** – To set the "background color" of the plot as white, use command "sns.set(style="whitegrid", color_codes=True)."

- **Step 4** – To set the "plot size" for all plots, use command "sns.set(rc={'figure.figsize':(11.7,8.27)})."

- **Step 5** – To generate a "countplot", use the command "sns.countplot('Route To Market', data=sales_data, hue = 'Opportunity Result')."

- **Step 6** – To remove the top and bottom margins, use the command

Python Programming

"sns.despine(offset=10, trim=True)."

- **Step 7** – To display the plot, use the command "plotplt.show()."

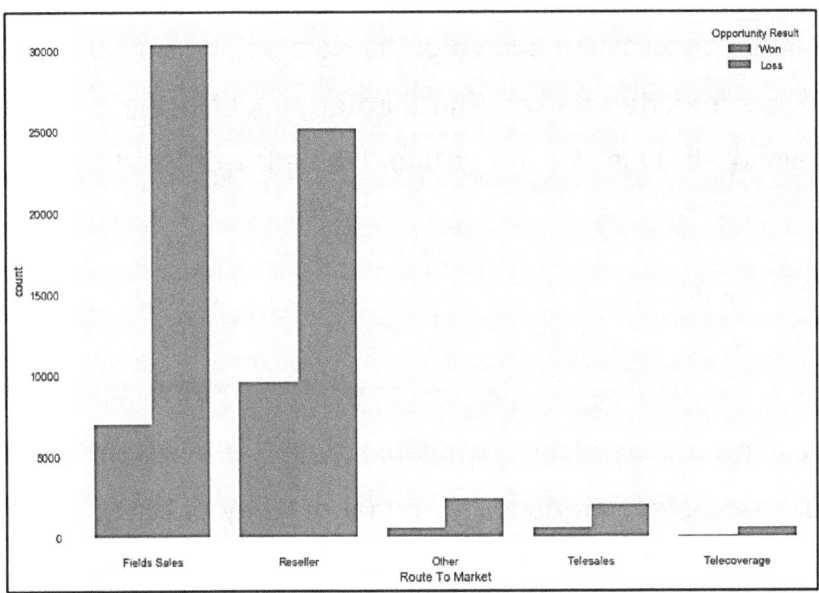

Quick Recap

The "Seaborn" and "Matplotlib" modules were imported first. Then the "set()" technique was used to define the distinct characteristics for our plots, such as plot style and color. The background of the plot was defined to be white using the code snippet "sns.set(style= "whitegrid", color codes= True)." Then the plot size was define using command "sns.set(rc={'figure.figsize':(11.7,8.27)})" that define the size of the plot as "11.7px and 8.27px."

Next the command "sns.countplot('Route To Market',data= sales data, hue='Opportunity Result')" was used to generate the plot. The "countplot()" technique enables the creation of a count plot, which can expose multiple arguments to customize the count plot according to our requirements. As part of the first "countplot()" argument, the X-axis was defined as the column "Route to Market" from the data set. The next argument concerns the source of the data set, which would be "sales_data" data framework we imported earlier. The third argument is the color of the bar graphs that were defined as "blue" for the column labeled "won" and "green" for the column labeled "loss."

Data Pre-processing

By now, you should have a clear understanding of what information is available in the data set. From the data exploration step, we established that majority of the columns in our data set are "string data", but "Scikit-Learn" can only process numerical data. Fortunately, the Scikit-Learn library offers us many ways to convert string data into numerical data, for example, "LabelEncoder()" technique. To transform categorical labels from the data set such as "won" and "loss" into numerical values, we will use the "LabelEncoder()" technique.

Let's look at the pictures below to see what we are attempting to accomplish with the "LabelEncoder()" technique. The first image contains one column labeled "color" with three records namely, "Red," "Green" and "Blue." Using the "LabelEncoder()" technique, the record in the same "color" column can be converted to numerical values, as shown in the second image.

	Color
0	1
1	2
2	3

Python Programming

	Color
0	Red
1	Green
2	Blue

Let's begin the real process of conversion now. Using the "fit transform()" technique given by "LabelEncoder()," the labels in the categorical column like "Route To Market" can be encoded and converted to numerical labels comparable to those shown in the diagrams above. The function "fit transform()" requires input labels identified by the user and consequently returns encoded labels.

To know how the encoding is accomplished, let's go through an example quickly. The code instance below constitutes string data in form of a list of cities such as ["Paris", "Paris", "Tokyo", "Amsterdam"] that will be encoded into something comparable to "[2, 2, 1,3]."

- **Step 1** – To import the required module, use the command "from sklearn import preprocessing."

- **Step 2** – To create the Label encoder object, use the command "le = preprocessing.LabelEncoder()."

- **Step 3** – To convert the categorical columns into numerical values, use the command: "encoded_value = le.fit_transform(["Paris", "Paris", "Tokyo", "Amsterdam"])" "print(encoded_value) [1 1 2 0]."

And there you have it! We just converted our string data labels into numerical values. The first step was importing the preprocessing module that offers the "LabelEncoder()" technique. Followed by the development of an object representing the "LabelEncoder()" type. Then the "fit_transform()" function of the object was used to distinguish between distinct classes of the list ["Paris", "Paris", "Tokyo", "Amsterdam"] and output the encoded values of "[1 1 20]."

Did you observe that the "LabelEncoder()" technique assigned the numerical values to the classes in alphabetical order according to the initial letter of the classes, for example "(A)msterdam" was assigned code "0", "(P)aris" was assigned code "1" and "(T)okyo" was assigned code "2."

Creating Training and Test subsets

To know the interactions between distinct characteristics and how these characteristics influence the target variable, a ML algorithm must be trained on a collection of information. We need to split the complete data set into two subsets to accomplish this. One subset will serve as the training data set, which will be used to train our algorithm to construct machine learning models. The other subset will serve as the test data set, which will be used to test the accuracy of the predictions generate by the machine learning model.

You probably feel very comfortable taking on some forms of data science after finishing this book. If you feel that excitement, then you are on the right track. However, there is still a need to plan well before delving into it.

Many things you will need to understand before you can achieve your goals and without the right plan, this will be virtually impossible. So make sure you get yourself a checklist before taking the leap. Trust me; it will be important in the long run.

Planning will also ensure that you know just what aspects of data science you like the most. Knowing this will ensure that you know what you are interested in as well as your strengths and your weaknesses heading into the newfound career.

- **Read more:** In this world of data science, reading will continue to be one important way of making sure that you keep advancing. Thanks to the internet, there are so many books which can help you to achieve your aim. So make sure that you are always reading and exploring new things and concepts. The only constant thing in the data science industry is that things are constantly changing with each passing day. So make sure that you stay on top of things.

- **Seek out the professional community:** Fortunately for you, there are a lot of experts out there who can be considered experts in all matters relating to data mining. While this book gives you the beginners' guide as you go deeper, you will need to gather some more experience. There is only so much experience, which you can get from reading books. You will eventually have to seek out the experts in the field. They provide some valuable tips, which you will probably not find in any books.

- **Practice every day:** You cannot become a great data scientist without actually putting in the work. You will need to work to develop yourself in the field every day. The truth is that with data science, there is always something new to learn and you will surely be doing yourself a world of good by practicing. Do you know the best part about practicing? It gets easier! Soon, you will be used to it and will be geared to go on with each passing year.

- **Take the Leap:** You're finally ready. Having cold feet? It is time for you to take the leap. You have already invested so much into learning the trade and it is time to kick off your career in data science. What if you are the owner of an organization looking for ways to make sure that your company gets the best data science and what it offers? Then. It is also time to take the leap and make sure your company keeps on reaping the fruits of the integration of data science into your business.

- **Get a job and keep networking:** There is so much more to explore out there. Keep working and expand your horizons past data science. All you need is a measure of confidence. Once you have that, the world will be at your feet.

The next step is to start putting some of the information we have discussed in this guidebook to good use. As a business, if you have not already started to collect data from various sources whether online, social media, from the customers who shop on your site, or more, then you are already falling behind. Only once that information is collected you can begin the real work of sorting through all of that data and figuring out some of the information hidden inside. This guidebook spent some time looking at this process, and all of the steps that you can take to make data science, with the help of the Python coding language, work for you.

This guidebook has provided us with a lot of different information on data science, how it works, machine learning, the Python language, and even some of the examples of how you can put all of this together and actually make it all work. Often data science sounds difficult and too hard to work on, but this guidebook has shown us some of the practical steps that we can take to put it all together.

When you are finally ready to take on some of the data that you have been accumulating and you are excited to make this all work for you in terms of providing better customer service, and really seeing some good results in the decisions that you make for your business, make sure to check out this guidebook to help you get started with Python for data science.

Finally, keep your head up! Being focused and learning more about data science will be the best decision you have made this year.

My effort in writing this manual has been so much, so I would be glad if you would leave a review for the work done!

www.ingramcontent.com/pod-product-compliance
Lightning Source LLC
Chambersburg PA
CBHW080450220526
45465CB00006B/2226